Betty Crocker's
GREAT MAIN DISHES WITHOUT MEAT

Betty Crocker's
GREAT MAIN DISHES WITHOUT MEAT

PRENTICE HALL

NEW YORK   LONDON   TORONTO   SYDNEY   TOKYO   SINGAPORE

PRENTICE HALL
15 Columbus Circle
New York, New York 10023

Copyright © 1994 by General Mills, Inc., Minneapolis, Minnesota

Library of Congress Cataloging-in-Publication Data
Betty Crocker's Great main dishes without meat.
p.   cm.
Includes index.
ISBN 0-671-88251-1
1. Entrées (Cookery)   2. Vegetarian cookery.   I. Title: Great main dishes without meat.
TX837.B49   1994   93-4528
641.5′636—dc20   CIP

Designed by Levavi & Levavi

Manufactured in the United States of America

10   9   8   7   6   5   4   3   2   1

First Edition

Contents

Introduction   vi

Meatless Basics   vii

CHAPTER **1**   **Soups, Stews and Chile**   1

CHAPTER **2**   **Casseroles**   31

CHAPTER **3**   **Easy Skillet Dishes and Stir-Fries**   59

CHAPTER **4**   **Quiches, Frittatas and Soufflés**   87

CHAPTER **5**   **Satisfying Salads**   103

CHAPTER **6**   **Pizza, Sandwiches and Breads**   119

Index   135

Introduction

More and more people are interested in finding appealing recipes for main dishes without meat. While there are some meatless dishes that have always been American favorites, such as macaroni and cheese, there is an exciting range of meatless dishes to be explored, and we have gathered the most enticing ones right here.

While wanting to limit meat in their diet, some people are concerned they will not get enough nutrients, and so are wary of meatless meals. In reality, well-planned meatless meals give you plenty of nutrients, as well as the protein you need for a balanced diet. You'll learn how to mix incomplete proteins to make a complete protein—rice and beans for example—as well as use other protein sources creatively.

Do you think meatless meals are boring and bland? Then you'll be pleasantly surprised! These recipes will delight you and your family, as well as please guests. Sample Pasta Torte, Vegetable Stew with Dill Dumplings, Anasazi Enchiladas, Spring Vegetable Paella, Polenta with Italian Vegetables—even Meatless "Meatball" Pizza! You'll find all the recipes you need for the various meals you cook, from quick skillet meals to company fare and hearty week-night casseroles.

And, if you are thinking about following a vegetarian diet, you'll find this book very useful. Besides the inventive meatless recipes, you'll find complete menu plans showing you how to follow a well-balanced, and delicious, meat-free eating plan.

Whether you want to eat meatless meals regularly, or just want to try them once or twice a week, you'll love the recipes here.

THE BETTY CROCKER EDITORS

Meatless Basics

Americans are consuming less red meat. Whether it's for variety's sake, health factors, economic, ethical or even environmental reasons, eating meatless meals is catching on. We're choosing to eat more complex carbohydrates from foods such as legumes (peas and beans), grains, pasta, rice, breads, cereals, fruits, vegetables, nuts and seeds. To help you achieve great-tasting, nutritious main dishes from a variety of meatless sources, we've created *Betty Crocker's Meatless Main Dishes*. This beginning guide will entice you to enjoy scores of meatless recipes, whether you just want to prepare a few meals without meat each week or are considering becoming a vegetarian. However, this is not meant to be a complete vegetarianism handbook, though it will be a useful resource. Our versatile recipes include a wide array of flavors, textures and colors, and incorporate dishes from some of the world's greatest cuisines such as Indian and Asian. We have made efforts to regulate sodium, saturated fat and cholesterol to keep these recipes in line with current nutrition and health trends.

Meatless Cuisine

Meatless meals provide many advantages to your eating plan. However, there are some potential pitfalls that can be avoided with a little extra care. Let's examine the nutritional attributes and other factors that affect meatless cuisine.

Cholesterol, which comes only from animal sources, and saturated fat, which also typically comes from animal foods, are the dietary components most often linked to elevated blood cholesterol and coronary heart disease. Decreasing the consumption of foods that significantly contribute saturated fat and cholesterol to our diets is recommended by nutrition and health experts. By eating more plant foods such as legumes, grains, pasta, breads, cereals, fruits, vegetables, nuts and seeds, dietary cholesterol and saturated fat intakes may be reduced.

Nutrition experts do not recommend that we refrain from eating red meat or any other food entirely. Small amounts of lean chicken and turkey, fish, and extra-lean cuts of beef may be used as accompaniments to many dishes in this book, if portions are small. For example, see Red Beans and Rice (page 33), Pasta Torte (page 48) or Greek Pasta Salad (page 110). You should keep an eye on the use of eggs and dairy products, as these foods contain some saturated fat and cholesterol and, if consumed indiscriminately, can be sources of extra calories.

Legumes, fruits, vegetables, nuts, seeds and certain grains and cereals provide the added benefit of dietary fiber. Dietary Guidelines for Americans tell us to increase our intake of fiber to 25 to 30 grams each day. Meatless meals help increase dietary fiber consumption, as plant foods provide more fiber per serving than do animal foods. Legumes, for example, generally provide at least 5 grams of dietary fiber per ½ cup serving, and many of our recipes supply a great deal more fiber. Increasing consumption of fruits and vegetables, raw or cooked, will add fiber to your diet, as will high-fiber breakfast cereals eaten as a meal in the morning or as a snack. Nuts and seeds provide fiber as well but should be eaten in moderation as the fat content of these foods is relatively high.

As you learn to prepare meatless meals, you may tend to substitute whole eggs and regular dairy items such as cheese for meat protein. This often results in your consuming more saturated fat and cholesterol than you realize. In an effort to help you limit fat and cholesterol, many of our recipes call for reduced-fat dairy products and egg substitutes. You still have the option to use regular dairy products and eggs—they are listed as alternative ingredients.

Increasing fiber can be a tricky business for certain individuals. It's best to start slowly so your body can adjust to the complex sugars, called oligosaccharides, that are found in legumes. It's the human body's inability to digest oligosaccharides that may cause gas, flatulence and even diarrhea in some people. Thoroughly draining the cooking liquid from canned beans and then rinsing them, or rinsing the soaking or cooking liquid from cooked, dried beans can help to eliminate most of the gaseous side effects. Also, over-the-counter remedies may ease the problem.

Vitamin and mineral deficiencies are potential problems for people who are true vegetarians and even for those who avoid red meat. But if your diet contains some animal foods, these deficiencies are less likely to develop.

Iron and zinc are two minerals that may be in jeopardy because the body does not absorb them as well from plant foods as from meat and dairy products. Dried beans, dried fruits, fortified breakfast cereals and breads are good plant sources of iron. Peas, lentils and wheat germ are good plant sources of zinc. Vitamin B_2 (riboflavin) and vitamin B_{12} deficiencies are possible when meat, dairy foods and eggs are eliminated from the diet.

Eating dairy products such as milk, yogurt and cheese, and certain dark green vegetables such as spinach and broccoli is important to meet calcium needs. Calcium is a nutrient of particular importance to women and children. The use of nonfat and low-fat versions of dairy items in recipes helps you choose calcium-rich sources for a diet that is lower in fat.

Protein for Life

We need protein for growth and maintenance of body tissues, and meatless foods can provide adequate protein. Proteins are made of building blocks called amino acids. Some of these amino acids can be manufactured in our bodies. The amino acids we cannot produce, called *essential amino acids*, must come directly from the foods we eat. Essential amino acids are the building blocks that best fit our needs. Proteins that contain all our essential amino acids, and therefore called *complete* or *high-quality* proteins, come from animal sources such as meats, eggs, chicken, fish and dairy products. Nonanimal protein sources such as legumes, grains, pasta, cereals, breads, nuts and seeds are *incomplete* or *lower-quality* proteins because the protein they provide is missing at least one of the essential amino acid building blocks.

Complementing Combinations

To ensure good-quality protein, we can combine low-quality proteins. This way, lesser-quality protein foods can *complement* or *complete* the amino acids missing from one food alone to create complete protein with the same quality as animal protein.

Grain foods complement legumes; legumes complement the mixture of nuts and seeds. The pairings are almost endless. Familiar examples of foods that provide high-quality protein include peanut butter on whole wheat bread, or a bean burrito (beans in a corn tortilla). By eating a low-quality protein food such as pasta with a high-quality protein, such as cheese, you create a meal with complete protein. Take a look at our complementary proteins chart (page ix). By mixing and matching foods from the first column with those in the second, you can create complete proteins in a great variety of ways.

Complementary protein foods do not have to be eaten in the same mouthful for you to reap the benefits of complete protein! Recent studies show that as long as you eat a variety of foods each day, you'll most likely eat enough complete protein to meet your needs. Learning how to complete protein sources is of great importance for vegetarians and for people who do not eat animal foods.

However, for most of us who eat a varied daily diet, protein completion is generally not a problem.

Planning Meatless Meals

Strive for variety, good taste and balanced nutrition when planning meatless meals. Experiment with herbs, spices and seasoning blends; try mixing hot and spicy flavors with cool and creamy or sweet ones. You can also vary cooked and raw ingredients in recipes to achieve interesting textures.

Use seasonal fresh ingredients whenever possible, but canned or frozen options are good alternatives. Try not to repeat ingredients in the dishes you serve at the same meal, to ensure your family gets an assortment of nutrients. Also, include complementary protein foods, or a high-quality protein food such as cheese or eggs, in meatless meals. Give free rein to your imagination and create many exciting, delicious combinations.

How to Use Nutrition Information

Nutrition information per serving for each recipe includes the amounts of calories, protein, carbohydrate, fat, cholesterol and sodium.

• If ingredient choices are given, the first listed ingredient is used in recipe nutrition information calculations.

• Cooked rice, pasta and vegetables, when called for as an ingredient, are unsalted.

• Two-percent milk is used to calculate the nutrition information wherever milk is listed in the ingredients.

• When ingredient ranges or more than one serving size is indicated, the first weight or serving is used to calculate nutrition information.

• "If desired" ingredients and recipe variations are not included in nutrition information calculations.

Mix and Match Complementary Protein Combinations

Mix and match foods from the first column with those in the second to achieve complete proteins.

LEGUMES	GRAINS, NUTS & SEEDS
kidney beans	corn bread
lentils	white or brown rice
navy beans	pasta
garbanzo beans (chick peas)	rye bread
pinto beans	cashews and sunflower nuts
black beans	corn or flour tortillas
tofu (bean curd)	tahini (sesame-seed paste)
lima beans	whole-grain rolls
peanuts or peanut butter	couscous
peas or split peas	whole-wheat pita bread
soybeans	barley
black-eyed peas	almonds and pumpkin seeds
cranberry beans	bulgur
adzuki beans	walnuts and sesame seeds
mung beans	wheat germ
Great Northern beans	oat bran muffin

Glossary

With the increase in meatless eating, new, unfamiliar ingredients are appearing more often in supermarkets, in food articles and on restaurant menus. The following list will help you become familiar with these new ingredients. Many are found in the recipes here, allowing you a good opportunity to give them a try.

Agar-Agar: This thickening agent is made from sea vegetation, and is used as a substitute for unflavored gelatin.

Anaheim Chiles (California green chiles): These chiles are slim, between five and eight inches long, and of various shades of light green. These mildly hot chiles are sometimes twisted in appearance.

Arborio Rice: Arborio is shorter, fatter and has a higher starch content than regular white rice. Originating in Italy, this rice is the preferred ingredient in risotto, where its starch contributes to risotto's creamy texture.

Arrowroot: This powdery starch comes from the tropical root of the same name, and is a substitute for cornstarch.

Barley Malt Syrup: This sweetener is made from sprouted whole barley. It has a mild caramel flavor and is not as sweet as sugar or honey.

Basmati Rice: Basmati is long-grained, fine-textured, aromatic and nutty-flavored rice that is often used in Indian and Middle Eastern cuisines.

Bok Choy (Chinese chard or white mustard cabbage): Bok choy has crisp, white stalks and shiny, dark green leaves. It is used primarily in soups and stir-fried dishes.

Brewer's Yeast: This yeast has no leavening power and is used in making beer. It is a good source of vitamin B and is widely consumed as a nutritional supplement.

Broc-o-flower: This vegetable, a cross between broccoli and cauliflower, has a pale, creamy green color.

Brown Rice Syrup: This sweetener is a cultured product made with brown rice, water and an enzyme. This syrup has a light flavor and is less sweet than sugar.

Carob: Carob is the dried pulp from the pods of the tropical carob tree. Carob is generally sold ground and is used as a substitute for cocoa powder.

Celeriac: Also known as celery root or celery knob, this root vegetable is very knobby in appearance and has a brown skin. With a flavor very similar to that of celery, it can be eaten raw or cooked.

Chile Oil: This red oil consists of vegetable oil in which chile peppers have been steeped to release their heat and flavor. It can be found in the International section of most large supermarkets.

Chile Paste: A hot, spicy sauce that is made from soybeans, hot peppers, salt, oil and garlic. It is used both in cooking and as a condiment. Chile paste can be found in the International section of most large supermarkets.

Chipotle Chiles in Adobo Sauce: Chipotles are smoked jalapeño peppers and are sold either dried (dried chipotles are brown and very wrinkled) or canned in a tomato-based sauce called adobo sauce.

Cilantro: Also known as Mexican parsley, Chinese parsley or fresh coriander. This herb resembles flat-leaf parsley, but the flavor is very different: strong, fresh and tangy.

Coconut Milk: Coconut milk is an unsweetened liquid made from a mixture of coconut meat that has been steeped in water, then strained. Sold canned, coconut milk is very rich and creamy, and the consistency can vary from quite thick to watery. It is primarily used in Indonesian cooking. Do not confuse coconut milk with cream-of-coconut or coconut cream. These sweetened products are primarily used in beverages and desserts.

Crème Fraîche: From France, this fermented cream has a slightly tangy, nutty flavor that resembles thinned sour cream, but is not as sour. It can be found in the dairy case of most large supermarkets and gourmet food stores. Crème fraîche is primarily used as a sauce. If unavailable, sour cream thinned with half-and-half can be used as a substitute.

Date Sugar: Fresh dates are more than 50 percent sugar, and that percentage increases as dates dry and the sugar becomes concentrated. Date sugar is made from dried dates with a high percentage of concentrated sugar.

Falafel: This Middle-Eastern speciality is a combination of ground garbanzo beans and a generous blend of spices. The mixture is formed into balls or patties and deep-fried, then served in pita bread with a yogurt sauce.

Fenugreek: Fenugreek is a seed known for its pleasantly bitter, slightly sweet flavor. Native to both Asia and southern Europe, fenugreek seeds or ground fenugreek is used to season many savory dishes and is an ingredient in some varieties of curry powder.

Garbanzo Flour: This flour is made of ground garbanzo beans and is a good source of protein.

Gluten Flour: Gluten flour is a high-protein flour that has been processed to remove most of its starch. It is used as an additive to doughs and to make bread, as gluten is necessary to make a light loaf.

Hoisin Sauce: This thick, sweet, reddish-brown sauce, usually made from soybeans, vinegar, chiles, spices and garlic, is used in cooking and as a condiment. It can be found in the International section of the grocery store.

Jalapeño Chiles: These chiles range from hot to very hot. They are dark green, fat and about two to three inches long with a characteristically rounded tip. Jalapeños ripen to red.

Jícama: The flesh of this root is often compared to that of the water chestnut, both for flavor (jícama is a little sweeter) and crunch. After the brown, fibrous skin has been peeled away, jícama flesh does not discolor.

Kalamata Olives: These purple-black olives, which are sold unpitted, are brine-cured in a wine or vinegar marinade. They are famous in Greek cuisine as well as in Middle Eastern and some Mediterranean cuisines. Kalamatas are fleshy, with a soft texture, and have a winelike flavor.

Kelp: Also known as kombu, it is an algae harvested from the ocean. Kelp is available in dried sheets and powdered, a form used as a salt substitute.

Kohlrabi: This vegetable bulb is a member of the turnip family, but it is milder and sweeter tasting. It can be eaten raw or cooked.

Lupini Pasta: A pasta made from the ground beans of the lupin plant, which has been cultivated for thousands of years. Lupini pasta contains more protein and fiber than regular pasta, and because of its very low starch content, it doesn't stick together and needs no rinsing.

Miso: Miso is a fermented paste made from soybeans and grain such as barley or rice. Ranging in color from yellow to red to brown, this paste is used primarily as a flavoring ingredient. It is commonly found in Japanese cooking.

Napa Cabbage: Also known as Chinese cabbage or celery cabbage, this oblong vegetable has pale green, very crinkled leaves.

Oyster Sauce: A thick, brown sauce made from oysters, salt, water and starch, it is used as an ingredient or table condiment. Oyster sauce can be found in the International section of the grocery store.

Nori: Nori is seaweed that has been dried in paper-thin sheets. Generally it is used for wrapping sushi and rice balls.

Pesto: A sauce found throughout Italy with many variations, but always with the same base—fresh basil, garlic and olive oil. It often has grated Parmesan or Romano cheese and pine nuts added. Pesto can be found in the grocery store in fresh and bottled forms.

Pine Nuts: Also called pinons and pignolis, they are the seeds of the pinon pine. Their delicate flavor is delicious raw or toasted. Store them tightly covered in the refrigerator or freezer.

Rice Wine: Also known as mirin, this golden, sweet wine is made from rice. Used extensively in Japanese cooking, it adds a subtle, sweet flavor. A light, sweet, white wine can be substituted for rice wine.

Seitan: This meat substitute is made by combining whole wheat flour and water. After the dough is mixed, it is repeatedly kneaded and rinsed while immersed in water to remove all of its starch. The resulting dough is then simmered twice in water or vegetable stock.

Serrano Chiles: These chiles are middling green in color, developing to a brilliant red when fully ripe. Extremely hot, this chile (commonly found in supermarkets) is usually shorter and thinner than the jalapeño.

Soba: Also known as Japanese noodles, soba are made from buckwheat flour and are dark brown in color.

Soy Grits: Soy grits are hulled, cracked soybeans. They can be cooked and eaten like the grits derived from corn served in the southern United States.

Soy Milk: Soy milk is made by pressing ground, cooked soybeans, and it is higher in protein than cow's milk. Because it is a nondairy product, it is a common substitute for those with milk allergies.

Sorghum: Sorghum is a cereal grass with clusters of grain on the top of each stalk. The grain itself is not used much in the United States. The plant stem yields a sweet juice that is boiled down into a syrup, and is often called sorghum molasses; true molasses, however, comes from sugar cane. Sorghum is used as a sweetener and table syrup.

Tahini: Also known as sesame seed paste, it comes from the Middle East and is made of ground sesame seeds. Tahini is an important addition to hummus, a classic Middle Eastern dip of pureed garbanzo beans.

Tamari: This soybean product is very similar in flavor to soy sauce, but is more subtle and a little bit thicker.

Tamarind Pulp: This comes from an intensely pungent, tart pod about 4 inches long. Tamarind is usually bought packaged with the entire pod tightly compressed and wrapped in plastic. The flesh is riddled with fibers and seeds and must be soaked before using. Separate the tamarind pods, pulling away and discarding as much of the pod as you reasonably can. Cover with water and let the pulp soak for at least an hour (overnight, if time permits). Then, squeeze the pulp well to extract the juice, or rub as much pulp as you can through a fine-mesh sieve. Grated lemon or lime peel can be used if tamarind is unavailable.

Tempeh: Tempeh is a soy product made by fermenting hulled, split soybeans and pressing them into cakes. Tempeh has a chewy texture and mild flavor. It is usually sold frozen.

Textured Vegetable Protein: Textured vegetable protein is a soy product packaged in either plain or seasoned, dehydrated form to which water is added, or in ready-to-use plain or seasoned products.

Tofu: Also known as soybean curd or bean curd, tofu is made from soybeans. The soybeans are soaked, cooked, ground and then mixed with a solidfying agent. The resulting curds are drained and pressed into cakes, which are tofu.

Tomatillos: These fat little vegetables are the size of robust cherry tomatoes. They grow in papery husks and taste best when they are brilliant green in color. Tomatillos have a very refreshing, acidic flavor. Select tomatillos with their light brown husks still drawn tightly around them. Husk and rinse off the sticky residue before using.

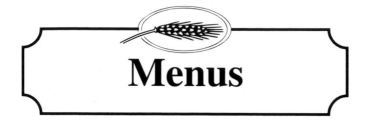

Menus

Casual entertaining with family and friends is replacing the formal dinner parties of the past. Why? As our leisure time lessens, our schedules become busier! However, this collection of nine delicious menus will fill your casual entertaining needs beautifully.

Serving brunch is a great way to get people together as well as a pleasant way to start the day. Our Spinach Frittata with Creole Sauce is reminiscent of the flavors of New Orleans, and when served with Quinoa Primavera Salad, fresh fruits and bagels, it is the perfect prelude to a day of outdoor activity such as cross-country or downhill skiing. For those who crave ethnic cuisine, we offer Curried Stew with Peanut Sauce. Pita bread wedges, along with cucumber and tomato slices, are perfect accompaniments; for a cooling and refreshing finale, there's low-fat frozen yogurt with low-fat butterscotch or fudge topping. In keeping with the theme of casual entertaining, you may want to have everyone contribute a dish to the meal, keeping things simple and fun!

FIRESIDE WEEKEND BRUNCH

Spinach Frittata with Creole Sauce (page 91)
Quinoa Primavera Salad (page 115)
Fruit platter
Assorted bagels
Preserves, cream cheese and peanut butter
Coffee or tea

EASY BRUNCH

Easy Oven Pancake (page 98)
Cinnamon-Nut Batter Bread (page 133)
Jam and jelly
Assorted raw vegetables, olives and pickles
Orange juice
Cookies
Coffee or tea

LIGHT BRUNCH

Swedish Summer Hash (page 82)
French toast and assorted syrups
Lemon-flavored angel food cake with fresh fruit
Coffee or tea

TEX-MEX LUNCH

Black Bean Taco Salad (page 104)
Calico Corn Muffins (page 132)
Hot cooked rice mixed with salsa
Sliced ripe olives and low-fat sour cream
Sangria, iced tea or lemonade

NEW ORLEANS PATIO LUNCH

Cajun Muffulettas (page 124)
Assorted snack chips and pretzels
Raw vegetable sticks
Fresh fruit
Iced tea or lemonade

ITALIAN TRATTORIA LUNCH

Tortellini, Bean and Pesto Soup (page 7)
Mixed greens with oil-and-vinegar dressing
Italian bread
Sorbet or fruit ice
Sparkling water

INDONESIAN DINNER

Curried Stew with Peanut Sauce (page 20)
Pita bread wedges
Cucumber and tomato slices
Frozen low-fat yogurt with low-fat but-
    terscotch and fudge topping
Sparkling water

PIZZA PARTY

Mediterranean Pizza (page 122)
Tossed salad with creamy cucumber dressing
    and croutons
Fresh fruit
Brownies and cookies
Sparkling water

MIDWINTER WARM-UP DINNER

Three-Bean White Chile (page 29)
Warm tortillas and corn muffins
Fat-free pound cake with berries and low-fat
    whipped topping
Beer, coffee, tea or low-fat milk

SPANISH SPRING LUNCH

Spring Vegetable Paella (page 69)
Savory Rosemary Scones (page 131)
Fresh Berries
Sangria, Sparkling water or iced tea

Menu Planning

Menu planning can be time consuming and difficult, but here we have done all the work for you! Seven days worth of meatless menus, each including breakfast, lunch and dinner, have all been carefully planned.

For a family-pleasing meal, try the delicious Italian Polenta Pizza. Its unique crust is made from a cooked mixture of cornmeal and milk with a touch of fresh Parmesan cheese; it is topped with a mild sauce and fresh vegetables. Chase away the winter chills by serving Bean and Pepper Chile with Calico Corn Muffins for lunch at home or on the job. If a menu for casual entertaining is in order, Mexican-food lovers will enjoy the Black Bean Enchiladas menu with salsa-spiked rice and corn with peppers.

You don't have to follow these menus in any particular order from day one to day seven; the order can be changed to suit your personal preferences as well as the ingredients available.

The nutrition information following each menu was calculated based on eating all three meals in that particular day's menu.

Day 1

Breakfast
½ grapefruit
1 serving Egg Burrito Grande (page 97)
1 cup low-fat milk
Coffee or tea

Lunch
1 carton (6 ounces) low-fat yogurt
1 plain bagel with 1 tablespoon jam
1 apple
Sparkling water

Dinner
1 serving Mushroom and Spinach Lasagne (page 51)
Mixed green salad with 1 tablespoon Italian dressing
2 slices whole wheat or white French bread
Fruit-flavored sorbet

Snack
3 ounces frozen low-fat yogurt
2 graham crackers

NUTRITION INFORMATION PER SERVING

ONE SERVING		PERCENT OF U.S. RDA	
Calories	1935	Vitamin A	98%
Protein, g	76	Vitamin C	100%
Carbohydrate, g	330	Calcium	100%
Fat, g	44	Iron	88%
Percent of Calories			
from Fat	20%		
Unsaturated	26		
Saturated	18		
Dietary fiber, g	22		
Cholesterol, mg	330		
Sodium, mg	3110		

Day 2

Breakfast
½ cup orange juice
¾ cup cooked oatmeal with cinnamon or multi-grain cereal with dried mixed fruits
1 slice raisin bread with 1 tablespoon peanut butter
1 cup low-fat milk

Lunch
1 serving Mixed Pepper and Bean Chile (page 36)
1 Calico Corn Muffin (page 132)
1 orange
1 cup low-fat milk

Dinner
1 serving Winter Baked Pasta (page 51)
Mixed greens salad with 1 tablespoon reduced-calorie French dressing
1 small whole-wheat dinner roll
Angel food cake with fresh or frozen strawberries and low-fat whipped topping

Snack
1 frozen gelatin pop
3 cups reduced-fat microwave popcorn

NUTRITION INFORMATION PER SERVING

ONE SERVING		PERCENT OF U.S. RDA	
Calories	1775	Vitamin A	100%
Protein, g	78	Vitamin C	100%
Carbohydrate, g	309	Calcium	100%
Fat, g	47	Iron	90%
Percent of Calories			
from Fat	24%		
Unsaturated	29		
Saturated	18		
Dietary fiber, g	35		
Cholesterol, mg	105		
Sodium, mg	3410		

Day 3

Breakfast
1 serving Fruited Gorgonzola and Cheddar Melts (page 124)
1 cup strawberries
Coffee or tea

Lunch
1 serving Kasha Tabbouleh (page 109)
1 whole wheat or white pita bread (6 inches in diameter)
1 orange
Sparkling water

Dinner
1 serving Black Bean Enchiladas (page 61)
Low-fat sour cream and salsa
1 cup cooked rice
½ cup Mexican-style corn

Snack
½ cup cinnamon-flavored applesauce
½ cup ice milk with 1 tablespoon caramel ice-cream topping

NUTRITION INFORMATION PER SERVING

ONE SERVING		PERCENT OF U.S. RDA	
Calories	1890	Vitamin A	76%
Protein, g	76	Vitamin C	100%
Carbohydrate, g	364	Calcium	100%
Fat, g	32	Iron	100%
Percent of Calories			
from Fat	15%		
Unsaturated	17		
Saturated	17		
Dietary fiber, g	39		
Cholesterol, mg	70		
Sodium, mg	3570		

Day 4

Breakfast
1 serving Asian Omelet (page 96)
½ cup pineapple chunks
1 slice Cinnamon-Nut Batter Bread (page 133)
Coffee or tea

Lunch
Mixed green salad with 1 tablespoon buttermilk
   salad dressing
1 serving Savory Walnut Hearth Bread (page 132)
¼ cantaloupe (5 inches)
1 cup low-fat milk

Dinner
1 serving Squash-and-Lentil Risotto (page 72)
1 cup cooked green beans
1 soft breadstick
Low-fat vanilla yogurt with fresh or frozen rasp-
   berries

Snack
1 apple
2 ounces fat-free pretzels

NUTRITION INFORMATION PER SERVING

ONE SERVING		PERCENT OF U.S. RDA	
Calories	1840	Vitamin A	100%
Protein, g	70	Vitamin C	100%
Carbohydrate, g	332	Calcium	96%
Fat, g	41	Iron	100%
Percent of Calories			
from Fat	20%		
Unsaturated	29		
Saturated	12		
Dietary fiber, g	34		
Cholesterol, mg	380		
Sodium, mg	3830		

Day 5

Breakfast
½ cup cranberry juice
½ cup bran cereal shreds
1 cup low-fat milk
1 banana (6 inches)

Lunch
1 serving Wild Rice and Spinach au Gratin
   (page 2)
1 serving Easy Brown Bread (page 133)
2 caramel-corn-flavored popcorn cakes
Sparkling water

Dinner
1 serving Polenta Pizza Casserole (page 120)
Mixed green salad with 1 tablespoon creamy Italian dressing and croutons
Fresh pineapple chunks and grapes
1 cup low-fat milk

Snack
1 frozen low-fat yogurt bar
1 raisin bagel with 2 teaspoons jam

NUTRITION INFORMATION PER SERVING

ONE SERVING		PERCENT OF U.S. RDA	
Calories	1885	Vitamin A	100%
Protein, g	74	Vitamin C	100%
Carbohydrate, g	301	Calcium	100%
Fat, g	54	Iron	80%
Percent of Calories			
from Fat	26%		
Unsaturated	27		
Saturated	27		
Dietary fiber, g	24		
Cholesterol, mg	120		
Sodium, mg	2690		

Day 6

Breakfast
1 serving "Egg-wich" (page 101)
½ cup orange juice
1 cup low-fat milk

Lunch
1 serving Green Jerked Chile (page 28)
1 cornbread muffin
Low-fat vanilla yogurt with kiwifruit
Iced tea

Dinner
1 serving Vegetable-Couscous Salad (page 112)
1 serving Savory Rosemary Scones (page 131)
¼ honeydew melon (5 inches)
1 cup low-fat milk

Snack
3 cups reduced-fat microwave popcorn

NUTRITION INFORMATION PER SERVING

ONE SERVING		PERCENT OF U.S. RDA	
Calories	1830	Vitamin A	100%
Protein, g	85	Vitamin C	100%
Carbohydrate, g	285	Calcium	100%
Fat, g	56	Iron	98%
Percent of Calories			
from Fat	28%		
Unsaturated	38		
Saturated	18		
Dietary fiber, g	37		
Cholesterol, mg	335		
Sodium, mg	3100		

Day 7

Breakfast
1 serving Rice and Bean Quiche (page 88)
1 cup strawberries
1 cup low-fat milk

Lunch
1 serving Pizza Soup (page 4)
Raw vegetable sticks with reduced-calorie butter-
    milk dressing
1 orange
1 cup low-fat milk

Dinner
1 serving Savory Bread Pudding (page 55)
1 cup cooked carrots
Fresh spinach tossed with sliced mushrooms, to-
    matoes and vinaigrette dressing
Frozen low-fat yogurt with crushed cereal and
    chocolate syrup

Snack
2 ounces fat-free pretzels
1 ounce raisins

NUTRITION INFORMATION PER SERVING

ONE SERVING		PERCENT OF U.S. RDA	
Calories	1820	Vitamin A	100%
Protein, g	92	Vitamin C	100%
Carbohydrate, g	305	Calcium	100%
Fat, g	45	Iron	100%
Percent of Calories			
from Fat	22%		
Unsaturated	27		
Saturated	18		
Dietary fiber, g	38		
Cholesterol, mg	160		
Sodium, mg	3870		

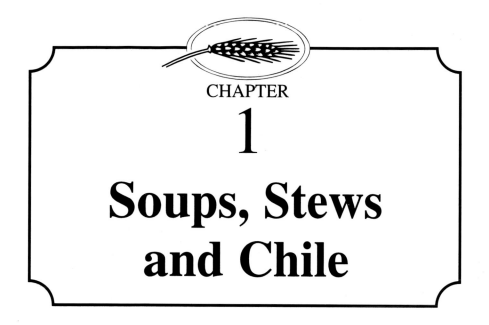

CHAPTER
1
Soups, Stews and Chile

While we often think of soups, stews and chiles as hearty winter fare, they are welcome all year long. When it's blustery outside, you'll enjoy sitting down to Tex-Mex Chile, and when it's warm and sultry, Gazpacho with Basil Crème Fraîche is just the thing. Would you like to add some homemade bread to your meal? Just turn to Chapter 6 (page 119) for easy, pleasing bread recipes. We think you'll find the zesty meals in this chapter turn an ordinary soup bowl into the main attraction!

Caribbean Stew with Pineapple Salsa (page 22)

Wild Rice and Spinach au Gratin

Jarlsberg is a buttery and rich, mildly flavored Swiss cheese. It's an excellent cheese for cooking because it melts so well.

> 2 cups chicken broth or Vegetable Broth (page 14)
> 1/2 cup uncooked wild or brown rice
> 3 cups shredded spinach (about 4 ounces)
> 1/4 cup all-purpose flour
> 3 cups milk
> 1 cup half-and-half
> 1/2 teaspoon onion powder
> 1/4 teaspoon ground nutmeg
> 1 1/2 cups shredded Jarlsberg or Swiss cheese (6 ounces)
> 2 tablespoons dry sherry or chicken broth

Heat broth and wild rice to boiling in 3-quart saucepan, stirring once or twice; reduce heat. Cover and simmer 40 to 50 minutes or until wild rice is tender; do not drain. Stir in spinach. Mix flour and milk until smooth; stir into soup. Stir in half-and-half, onion powder and nutmeg. Cook over medium heat, stirring constantly, until mixture thickens and boils; remove from heat. Stir in cheese and sherry; continue stirring until cheese in melted. Do not boil. *5 servings*

NUTRITION INFORMATION PER SERVING

ONE SERVING		PERCENT OF U.S. RDA	
Calories	360	Vitamin A	66%
Protein, g	20	Vitamin C	14%
Carbohydrate, g	32	Calcium	46%
Fat, g	18	Iron	10%
Unsaturated	7		
Saturated	11		
Dietary fiber, g	2		
Cholesterol, mg	55		
Sodium, mg	740		

Santa Fe Corn Chowder

> 1/2 cup chopped onion (about 1 medium)
> 2 tablespoons margarine or butter
> 3 tablespoons all-purpose flour
> 3/4 teaspoon ground cumin
> 1/2 teaspoon garlic salt
> 1/2 teaspoon ground coriander
> 4 cups milk
> 1 package (16 ounces) frozen corn with red and green peppers
> 1 can (15 ounces) black beans, rinsed and drained
> 1 1/2 cups shredded sharp Cheddar cheese (6 ounces)
> 2 tablespoons chopped fresh cilantro

Cook onion in margarine in Dutch oven over medium heat about 5 minutes, stirring occasionally, until onion is crisp-tender. Mix flour, cumin, garlic salt and coriander in medium bowl; gradually stir in milk. Pour into Dutch oven. Stir in corn and beans. Heat to boiling, stirring constantly. Boil and stir 1 minute; remove from heat.

Stir in 1 cup of the cheese until melted. Top each serving with remaining cheese and the cilantro. *5 servings*

NUTRITION INFORMATION PER SERVING

ONE SERVING		PERCENT OF U.S. RDA	
Calories	470	Vitamin A	26%
Protein, g	26	Vitamin C	12%
Carbohydrate, g	55	Calcium	48%
Fat, g	20	Iron	18%
Unsaturated	9		
Saturated	11		
Dietary fiber, g	9		
Cholesterol, mg	50		
Sodium, mg	880		

Southern Lentils and Vegetables

1¼ cups dried lentils

1 cup sliced carrots (about 2 medium)

1 cup fresh or frozen green beans, cut into 1-inch pieces

½ cup chopped green onions (about 5 medium)

½ cup water

1 teaspoon Creole or Cajun seasoning

2 to 3 teaspoons red pepper sauce

⅛ teaspoon pepper

1 can (28 ounces) whole tomatoes, undrained

1 can (15 to 16 ounces) black-eyed peas, undrained

2 large sweet potatoes (about 1½ pounds), cut into 1-inch pieces

Heat all ingredients to boiling in Dutch oven, breaking up tomatoes; reduce heat. Cover and simmer 40 to 50 minutes or until vegetables and lentils are tender. *6 servings*

NUTRITION INFORMATION PER SERVING

ONE SERVING		PERCENT OF U.S. RDA	
Calories	270	Vitamin A	100%
Protein, g	19	Vitamin C	34%
Carbohydrate, g	63	Calcium	10%
Fat, g	1	Iron	40%
Unsaturated	1		
Saturated	0		
Dietary fiber, g	17		
Cholesterol, mg	0		
Sodium, mg	410		

Pizza Soup

1 medium onion, sliced

*1 large red bell pepper, cut into 1-inch
pieces*

*1 large green bell pepper, cut into 1-inch
pieces*

2 cloves garlic, finely chopped

1 tablespoon olive or vegetable oil

2 cups water

*2 cans (14¹/₂ ounces each) diced tomatoes
in olive oil, garlic and spices,
undrained*

1 can (6 ounces) tomato paste

1 cup sliced mushrooms (about 3 ounces)

1¹/₂ teaspoons Italian seasoning, crumbled

1 teaspoon fennel seed

*1 can (15 to 16 ounces) kidney beans,
rinsed and drained*

*1 can (15 to 16 ounces) cannellini beans,
rinsed and drained*

6 slices French bread, each ¹/₂ inch thick

*1¹/₂ cups shredded part-skim or regular
mozzarella cheese (6 ounces)*

Cook onion, bell peppers and garlic in oil in Dutch oven, stirring occasionally, until onion is tender. Stir in water, tomatoes and tomato paste until blended. Stir in remaining ingredients except bread and cheese. Heat to boiling; reduce heat. Cover and simmer 10 minutes, stirring occasionally.

Just before serving, heat oven to 425°. Place bread on ungreased cookie sheet. Toast bread in oven about 6 minutes, turning once, until golden brown. Set oven control to broil. Pour hot soup into 6 ovenproof soup bowls or casseroles. Top each with 1 slice toast. Sprinkle with cheese. Broil soup with tops 3 to 4 inches from heat 1 to 2 minutes or until cheese is melted. *6 servings*

NUTRITION INFORMATION PER SERVING

ONE SERVING		PERCENT OF U.S. RDA	
Calories	370	Vitamin A	30%
Protein, g	25	Vitamin C	68%
Carbohydrate, g	62	Calcium	32%
Fat, g	9	Iron	38%
Unsaturated	5		
Saturated	4		
Dietary fiber, g	15		
Cholesterol, mg	15		
Sodium, mg	1080		

Pizza Soup

Tortellini, Bean and Pesto Soup

1 clove garlic, finely chopped

1 medium carrot, cut into julienne strips

$\frac{1}{2}$ cup chopped onion (about 1 medium)

$\frac{1}{2}$ cup chopped celery (about 1 medium stalk)

2 tablespoons margarine or butter

6 cups water

2 teaspoons chicken bouillon granules

1 can (15 to 16 ounces) kidney beans, rinsed and drained

1 package (10 ounces) dried cheese-filled tortellini (about 2$\frac{1}{2}$ cups)

1 tablespoon chopped fresh parsley

$\frac{1}{4}$ teaspoon pepper

6 tablespoons pesto

6 tablespoons freshly grated Parmesan cheese

Cover and cook garlic, carrot, onion and celery in margarine in Dutch oven over medium-low heat 10 minutes, stirring frequently. Stir in water and bouillon granules. Heat to boiling; reduce heat. Stir in beans and tortellini.

Cover and simmer 20 minutes, stirring occasionally, until tortellini are tender. Stir in parsley and pepper. Top each serving with pesto and cheese. Serve immediately. *6 servings*

NUTRITION INFORMATION PER SERVING

ONE SERVING		PERCENT OF U.S. RDA	
Calories	370	Vitamin A	24%
Protein, g	16	Vitamin C	4%
Carbohydrate, g	57	Calcium	14%
Fat, g	12	Iron	24%
Unsaturated	9		
Saturated	3		
Dietary fiber, g	8		
Cholesterol, mg	5		
Sodium, mg	610		

Southern Lentils and Vegetables (page 3), Tortellini, Bean and Pesto Soup

Southwestern Black Bean Soup

Tequila adds a flavorful twist here, and the toppings bring an appealing array of tastes and textures to this hearty soup.

3 cups chicken broth or Vegetable Broth (page 14)

2 cups water

1 cup dried black beans

1 tablespoon chile powder

1 teaspoon ground cumin

¹/₄ teaspoon crushed red pepper

¹/₄ teaspoon salt

2 cloves garlic, finely chopped

1 to 2 jalapeño chiles, finely chopped

1 cup chopped onion (about 1 large)

¹/₂ cup sliced carrot (about 1 medium)

1 cup chopped celery (about 2 medium stalks)

¹/₄ cup tequila, if desired

¹/₄ cup shredded Cheddar cheese (1 ounce)

¹/₄ cup diced jícama

1 small avocado, peeled and cubed

1 small tomato, seeded and chopped

Heat broth, water and beans to boiling in Dutch oven. Boil uncovered 2 minutes; remove from heat. Cover and let stand 1 hour.

Heat beans to boiling again; reduce heat. Cover and simmer about 2 hours or until beans are tender. Stir in chile powder, cumin, red pepper, salt, garlic, chiles, onion, carrot, celery and tequila. Cover and simmer 1 hour. Place soup in blender or food processor. Cover and blend or process until of uniform consistency. Serve with cheese, jícama, avocado and tomato. *4 servings*

NUTRITION INFORMATION PER SERVING

ONE SERVING		PERCENT OF U.S. RDA	
Calories	305	Vitamin A	44%
Protein, g	18	Vitamin C	32%
Carbohydrate, g	46	Calcium	16%
Fat, g	11	Iron	28%
Unsaturated	8		
Saturated	3		
Dietary fiber, g	13		
Cholesterol, mg	5		
Sodium, mg	820		

Cabbage-Bean Soup with Rivels

Rivels are found in Amish and Mennonite cooking, and are similar to the German spaetzle. Rivels are tiny noodles or dumplings made from flour, eggs and milk or water.

Rivels (right)

5 cups shredded green cabbage (about ¹/₂ head)

1¹/₃ cups shredded carrots (about 2 medium)

1 cup chopped onion (about 1 large)

1 cup coarsely chopped apple (about 1 medium)

4 cups water

2 tablespoons bacon-flavored chips or bits

1 tablespoon chicken bouillon granules

1 tablespoon cider vinegar

1 teaspoon caraway seed

¹/₂ teaspoon salt

¹/₄ teaspoon pepper

1 can (15 to 16 ounces) great northern beans, rinsed and drained

Prepare Rivels; reserve. Heat remaining ingredients to boiling in Dutch oven; reduce heat. Add Rivels, stirring to separate. Cover and simmer 15 to 20 minutes, stirring occasionally, until vegetables are tender. *6 servings*

RIVELS

1 cup all-purpose flour

2 tablespoons milk

1 egg, beaten

Mix flour, milk and egg, using 2 forks, until particles are size of raisins.

NUTRITION INFORMATION PER SERVING

ONE SERVING		PERCENT OF U.S. RDA	
Calories	230	Vitamin A	40%
Protein, g	12	Vitamin C	34%
Carbohydrate, g	47	Calcium	12%
Fat, g	3	Iron	24%
Unsaturated	2		
Saturated	1		
Dietary fiber, g	8		
Cholesterol, mg	35		
Sodium, mg	420		

Cooking Dried Legumes

To Soak or Not To Soak before Cooking

Recent findings indicate that all legumes except lentils should be boiled uncovered for 2 minutes before cooking. This destroys an enzyme that can cause some people to become ill. This boiling time eliminates the need for the traditional, long-soaking method to help rehydrate legumes. Although an 8- to 24-hour soaking is not necessary, it does allow for more uniform swelling of legumes. If you choose to soak legumes before cooking, use one of the following methods:

Long-soak Method: Place legumes in large saucepan or bowl in enough cold water to cover. Let stand at least 8 hours or overnight. Drain and rinse. Boil beans 2 minutes in enough water to cover. Drain water if desired.

Quick-soak Method: Boil beans 2 minutes in enough water to cover. Remove from heat; cover and let stand 1 hour before cooking. Drain water if desired.

Selection, Storage and Cooking Tips

• When purchasing legumes, look for bright, uniform color and smooth, unbroken seed coats, as they indicate good quality and freshness. Uniform size results in even cooking.

• Store dry legumes in an airtight container in a cool, dry location.

• Sort legumes before cooking to remove any damaged beans or foreign matter.

• Beans of similar size can easily be interchanged in recipes.

• Dried legumes double or triple in volume as they cook, so be sure to use a sufficiently large pan or casserole.

• To prevent beans from foaming when cooking, add 1 tablespoon margarine or vegetable oil to the cooking water; drain and rinse.

• Salt and acid tend to toughen beans. Add salt and acidic foods such as lemon juice, vinegar, tomatoes and tomato sauce, paste or juice only after the beans are soft, or the beans may not soften.

• High altitude and hard water may increase cooking times.

• Beans get drier with age, and old beans may take longer to cook. Very old beans may never soften completely.

• Simmer, rather than boil, beans to avoid bursting the bean skins.

• Bean cooking liquid, which has minimal nutritional value, can be discarded, if desired. Or it can be saved and included as a part of the liquid necessary for a recipe.

• Store cooked beans in the refrigerator for 2 to 3 days or freeze as long as 8 months.

Legume Cooking Chart

Legumes lose moisture with age, so you may find that you need more water than the recipe calls for. If all the water is absorbed but the legume isn't quite tender, add a little more water and cook longer. If it is tender but all the water hasn't been absorbed, drain if desired.

TYPE OF DRY BEAN	AMOUNT OF WATER	METHOD OF COOKING (USING 3- TO 4-QUART SAUCEPAN)	APPROXIMATE COOKING TIME	APPROXIMATE YIELD
Adzuki (1 cup)	Enough to cover beans.	Heat water and beans to a boil. Boil uncovered 2 minutes; reduce heat. Cover and simmer.	30 to 45 minutes	3 cups
Anasazi (1 cup)	Enough to cover beans.	Heat water and beans to a boil. Boil uncovered 2 minutes; reduce heat. Cover and simmer.	1 to 2 hours	2 cups
Black (1 cup)	Enough to cover beans.	Heat water and beans to a boil. Boil uncovered 2 minutes; reduce heat. Cover and simmer.	1 to 2 hours	2 cups
Black-eyed Peas (1 cup)	Enough to cover beans.	Heat water and beans to a boil. Boil uncovered 2 minutes; reduce heat. Cover and simmer.	1 to 1½ hours	2 cups
Butter Beans (1 cup)	Enough to cover beans.	Heat water and beans to a boil. Boil uncovered 2 minutes; reduce heat. Cover and simmer.	1 to 1½ hours	2 to 2¼ cups

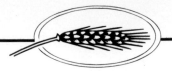

Legume Cooking Chart (*continued*)

TYPE OF DRY BEAN	AMOUNT OF WATER	METHOD OF COOKING (USING 3- TO 4-QUART SAUCEPAN)	APPROXIMATE COOKING TIME	APPROXIMATE YIELD
Cannellini (1 cup)	Enough to cover beans.	Heat water and beans to a boil. Boil uncovered 2 minutes; reduce heat. Cover and simmer.	1 to 1½ hours	2 to 2½ cups
Fava (1 cup)	Enough to cover beans.	Heat water and beans to a boil. Boil uncovered 2 minutes; reduce heat. Cover and simmer.	1 to 2 hours	2 cups
Garbanzo (1 cup)	Enough to cover beans.	Heat water and beans to a boil. Boil uncovered 2 minutes; reduce heat. Cover and simmer.	2 to 2½ hours	2 cups
Great Northern (1 cup)	Enough to cover beans.	Heat water and beans to a boil. Boil uncovered 2 minutes; reduce heat. Cover and simmer.	1 to 1½ hours	2 to 3 cups
Kidney (1 cup)	Enough to cover beans.	Heat water and beans to a boil. Boil uncovered 2 minutes; reduce heat. Cover and simmer.	1 to 2 hours	2 to 2½ cups
Lentils (1 cup)	Enough to cover lentils.	Heat water and lentils to a boil. Reduce heat. Cover and simmer.	30 to 45 minutes	2 to 2¼ cups

TYPE OF DRY BEAN	AMOUNT OF WATER	METHOD OF COOKING (USING 3- TO 4-QUART SAUCEPAN)	APPROXIMATE COOKING TIME	APPROXIMATE YIELD
Lima (1 cup)	Enough to cover beans.	Heat water and beans to a boil. Boil uncovered 2 minutes; reduce heat. Cover and simmer.	1 to 1½ hours	2 cups
Mung (1 cup)	Enough to cover beans.	Heat water and beans to a boil. Boil uncovered 2 minutes; reduce heat. Cover and simmer.	45 to 60 minutes	2 cups
Navy Beans (1 cup)	Enough to cover beans.	Heat water and beans to a boil. Boil uncovered 2 minutes; reduce heat. Cover and simmer.	1½ to 2 hours	2 cups
Pinto (1 cup)	Enough to cover beans.	Heat water and beans to a boil. Boil uncovered 2 minutes; reduce heat. Cover and simmer.	1½ to 2 hours	2 to 2½ cups
Soy (1 cup)	Enough to cover beans.	Heat water and beans to a boil. Boil uncovered 2 minutes; reduce heat. Cover and simmer.	3 to 4 hours	2 cups
Split Peas (1 cup)	Enough to cover split peas.	Heat water and beans to a boil. Boil uncovered 2 minutes; reduce heat. Cover and simmer.	45 to 60 minutes	2¼ cups

Mediterranean Vegetable Soup

1 tablespoon margarine or butter

1 tablespoon olive or vegetable oil

1 cup chopped onion (about 1 large)

1/2 cup chopped carrot (about 1 medium)

1/2 cup chopped celery (about 1 medium stalk)

4 cloves garlic, finely chopped

2 cups cubed eggplant

1 cup chopped pitted prunes

1/2 cup pimiento-stuffed olives

1/3 cup packed brown sugar

4 cups chicken broth or Roasted Vegetable Broth (right)

2 cups dry red wine, chicken broth or Roasted Vegetable Broth (page 15)

1 tablespoon capers, drained

2 teaspoons chopped fresh or 1/2 teaspoon dried oregano leaves

1 teaspoon chopped fresh or 1/4 teaspoon dried sage leaves

1 can (15 to 16 ounces) great northern beans, rinsed and drained

2 bay leaves

6 cups hot cooked Arborio, basmati or brown rice

Heat margarine and oil in Dutch oven over medium-high heat. Cook onion, carrot, celery and garlic in oil mixture 5 minutes, stirring occasionally. Stir in remaining ingredients except rice. Heat to boiling; reduce heat. Simmer uncovered 20 to 30 minutes, stirring occasionally, until vegetables are tender. Remove bay leaves.

Place 1 cup rice in each of 6 large soup bowls or casseroles. Ladle soup over rice. *6 servings*

NUTRITION INFORMATION PER SERVING

ONE SERVING		PERCENT OF U.S. RDA	
Calories	505	Vitamin A	22%
Protein, g	17	Vitamin C	4%
Carbohydrate, g	100	Calcium	14%
Fat, g	9	Iron	30%
Unsaturated	7		
Saturated	2		
Dietary fiber, g	11		
Cholesterol, mg	0		
Sodium, mg	1580		

Vegetable Broth

Fresh vegetable broth is easily made at home using vegetables that you most likely have in your refrigerator or pantry. Although not a meal in itself, this versatile broth serves as a base for many recipes in this book.

6 cups coarsely chopped mild vegetables (bell peppers, carrots, celery, leeks, mushroom stems, potatoes, spinach, zucchini)

1/2 cup coarsely chopped onion (about 1 medium)

1/2 cup parsley sprigs

8 cups cold water

2 sprigs basil or 2 teaspoons dried basil leaves

2 sprigs thyme or 2 teaspoons dried thyme leaves

1 teaspoon salt

1/4 teaspoon cracked black pepper

4 cloves garlic, chopped

2 bay leaves

Heat all ingredients to boiling in Dutch oven or stockpot; reduce heat. Cover and simmer 1 hour, stirring occasionally. Cool slightly. Strain and refrigerate up to 3 days.* Stir before measuring. *About 8 cups broth*

Note: Some strong vegetables, such as broccoli, cabbage, cauliflower, turnips and rutabagas, may be used sparingly with mild vegetables.

* Broth can be frozen.

NUTRITION INFORMATION PER SERVING

ONE SERVING		PERCENT OF U.S. RDA	
Calories	5	Vitamin A	*
Protein, g	0	Vitamin C	*
Carbohydrate, g	1	Calcium	*
Fat, g	0	Iron	*
Unsaturated	0		
Saturated	0		
Dietary fiber, g	0		
Cholesterol, mg	0		
Sodium, mg	270		

Roasted Vegetable Broth

6 cups large pieces mild vegetables (carrots, celery, whole mushrooms, potatoes and sweet potatoes)

2 medium onions, cut into fourths

2 cloves garlic, peeled

8 cups cold water

1/2 cup parsley sprigs

1 sprig basil or 1 teaspoon dried basil leaves

1 sprig marjoram or 1 teaspoon dried marjoram leaves

1 sprig thyme or 1 teaspoon dried thyme leaves

1 teaspoon salt

1/4 teaspoon cracked black pepper

1 bay leaf

Heat oven to 400°. Grease jelly roll pan, 15½×10½×1 inch. Arrange vegetables, onions and garlic in pan. Bake 45 to 60 minutes or until vegetables are deep golden brown. Remove vegetables and place in Dutch oven or stockpot. Pour ½ cup of the cold water in pan. Scrape pan to remove browned particles; add water and particles to vegetables.

Heat vegetables, remaining cold water and remaining ingredients to boiling in Dutch oven; reduce heat. Cover and simmer 1 hour, stirring occasionally. Cool slightly. Strain and refrigerate up to 3 days.* Stir before measuring. *About 5 cups broth*

* Broth can be frozen.

NUTRITION INFORMATION PER SERVING

ONE SERVING		PERCENT OF U.S. RDA	
Calories	100	Vitamin A	100%
Protein, g	3	Vitamin C	40%
Carbohydrate, g	25	Calcium	6%
Fat, g	1	Iron	10%
Unsaturated	1		
Saturated	0		
Dietary fiber, g	5		
Cholesterol, mg	0		
Sodium, mg	500		

Gazpacho with Basil Crème Fraîche

2 cups chopped seeded tomatoes (*about 2 large*)

1¹/₂ cups chopped red bell pepper (*about 1 large*)

1 cup chopped peeled cucumber (*about 1 medium*)

¹/₂ cup diagonally sliced celery (*about 1 medium stalk*)

¹/₄ cup sliced green onions (*2 to 3 medium*)

2 cups tomato juice

2 tablespoons red wine vinegar

1 to 2 teaspoons red pepper sauce

¹/₄ teaspoon freshly ground pepper

¹/₄ teaspoon Worcestershire sauce

1 small clove garlic, finely chopped

1 can (*15 ounces*) black beans, rinsed and drained

Basil Crème Fraîche (*right*)

¹/₄ cup herb-flavored croutons, if desired

Mix all ingredients except Basil Crème Fraîche and croutons. Cover and refrigerate 4 to 6 hours to blend flavors, stirring occasionally.

Top each serving with Basil Crème Fraîche and croutons. *4 servings*

BASIL CRÈME FRAÎCHE

¹/₃ cup crème fraîche or sour cream

2 tablespoons chopped fresh or 1 teaspoon dried basil leaves

Mix ingredients.

NUTRITION INFORMATION PER SERVING

ONE SERVING		PERCENT OF U.S. RDA	
Calories	220	Vitamin A	30%
Protein, g	12	Vitamin C	76%
Carbohydrate, g	42	Calcium	14%
Fat, g	5	Iron	24%
Unsaturated	2		
Saturated	3		
Dietary fiber, g	10		
Cholesterol, mg	15		
Sodium, mg	730		

Gazpacho with Basil Crème Fraîche

Curried Yellow Split Pea Soup with Cilantro Cream

This soup combines Thai and Indian cuisines with delightful results. Be sure to use coconut milk, which is unsweetened, not the coconut cream product commonly used in frozen beverages.

> 1½ cups chopped red bell pepper (about 1 large)
>
> 1 cup chopped onion (about 1 large)
>
> 1 cup diced carrot (about 1 large)
>
> 1 teaspoon finely chopped gingerroot
>
> 2 cloves garlic, finely chopped
>
> 1 to 2 red jalapeño chiles, seeded and chopped
>
> 1 tablespoon hot chile oil or vegetable oil
>
> 1¼ cups dried yellow split peas
>
> 2 cups chicken broth or Vegetable Broth (page 14)
>
> 1 tablespoon curry powder
>
> ½ teaspoon salt
>
> 2 medium potatoes, peeled and cut into 1-inch cubes
>
> 1 can (14 ounces) coconut milk
>
> Cilantro Cream (below)

Cook bell pepper, onion, carrot, gingerroot, garlic and chiles in oil in 3-quart saucepan, stirring occasionally, until onion is tender. Stir in remaining ingredients except Cilantro Cream. Heat to boiling; reduce heat.

Cover and simmer 25 to 35 minutes or until peas and potatoes are tender. Top each serving with Cilantro Cream. *4 servings*

CILANTRO CREAM

> ⅓ cup plain yogurt
>
> 2 tablespoons chopped fresh cilantro
>
> ¼ teaspoon grated lime peel

Mix all ingredients.

NUTRITION INFORMATION PER SERVING

ONE SERVING		PERCENT OF U.S. RDA	
Calories	560	Vitamin A	68%
Protein, g	23	Vitamin C	70%
Carbohydrate, g	65	Calcium	12%
Fat, g	20	Iron	38%
Unsaturated	7		
Saturated	13		
Dietary fiber, g	9		
Cholesterol, mg	0		
Sodium, mg	700		

Lentil-Spinach Soup

> 2 medium onions, sliced
>
> 1 clove garlic, finely chopped
>
> 2 tablespoons olive or vegetable oil
>
> 1¼ cups dried lentils
>
> 3 cups water
>
> 1 teaspoon salt
>
> 4 cups chopped spinach (about 6 ounces) or 1 package (10 ounces) frozen chopped spinach, thawed and drained
>
> 1 teaspoon grated lemon peel
>
> 2 teaspoons lemon juice

Cook onions and garlic in oil in 3-quart saucepan over medium heat, stirring occasionally, until onions are tender. Stir in lentils, water and salt. Heat to boiling; reduce heat. Cover and simmer 1 hour. Stir in spinach, lemon peel and lemon juice. Cover and simmer about 5 minutes or until spinach is tender. *4 servings*

NUTRITION INFORMATION PER SERVING

ONE SERVING		PERCENT OF U.S. RDA	
Calories	280	Vitamin A	76%
Protein, g	19	Vitamin C	30%
Carbohydrate, g	45	Calcium	18%
Fat, g	8	Iron	40%
Unsaturated	7		
Saturated	1		
Dietary fiber, g	12		
Cholesterol, mg	0		
Sodium, mg	620		

Easy Baked Stew

*4 frozen soybean-based vegetable burgers,
thawed and cut into 1-inch pieces*

2 cups cubed potatoes (about 2 medium)

2 small turnips, peeled and cubed

1/2 rutabaga, cubed

*1 cup sliced celery (about 2 medium
stalks)*

1 cup sliced carrots (about 2 medium)

1/2 cup all-purpose flour

*2 cups Roasted Vegetable Broth (page 15)
or beef broth*

*2 tablespoons chopped fresh or 3/4
teaspoon dried thyme leaves*

*2 tablespoons chopped fresh or 3/4
teaspoon dried marjoram leaves*

1/4 teaspoon salt

1/4 teaspoon pepper

1 bay leaf

*1 can (16 ounces) whole tomatoes,
undrained*

3 small onions, cut into fourths

Heat oven to 350°. Mix burgers, potatoes, turnips, rutabaga, celery and carrots in Dutch oven. Mix flour and broth until smooth. Stir broth mixture and remaining ingredients into vegetable mixture, breaking up tomatoes. Heat to boiling over medium-high heat. Cover and bake 50 to 60 minutes, stirring occasionally, until vegetables are tender. Remove bay leaf. *4 servings*

NUTRITION INFORMATION PER SERVING

ONE SERVING		PERCENT OF U.S. RDA	
Calories	270	Vitamin A	74%
Protein, g	22	Vitamin C	50%
Carbohydrate, g	36	Calcium	20%
Fat, g	6	Iron	34%
Unsaturated	4		
Saturated	2		
Dietary fiber, g	4		
Cholesterol, mg	0		
Sodium, mg	1215		

Lentil and Vegetable Stew

3 cups water

1 1/4 cups dried lentils

1/2 cup chopped onion (about 1 medium)

*1/2 cup chopped celery (about 1 medium
stalk)*

1 tablespoon chopped fresh parsley

1 tablespoon beef bouillon granules

1 teaspoon salt

1 teaspoon ground cumin

2 medium potatoes, cut into 1-inch cubes

2 cloves garlic, finely chopped

2 medium zucchini, cut into 1/2-inch slices

Lemon wedges

Heat water and lentils to boiling in Dutch oven; reduce heat. Cover and simmer about 30 minutes or until lentils are almost tender. Stir in remaining ingredients except zucchini and lemon wedges. Cover and cook about 20 minutes or until potatoes are tender. Stir in zucchini. Cover and cook 10 to 15 minutes or until zucchini is tender. Serve with lemon wedges. *4 servings*

NUTRITION INFORMATION PER SERVING

ONE SERVING		PERCENT OF U.S. RDA	
Calories	260	Vitamin A	2%
Protein, g	18	Vitamin C	28%
Carbohydrate, g	57	Calcium	8%
Fat, g	1	Iron	40%
Unsaturated	1		
Saturated	0		
Dietary fiber, g	12		
Cholesterol, mg	0		
Sodium, mg	1510		

Spicy Black Bean Stew

4¹/₂ cups water

1 cup dried black beans

¹/₂ cup uncooked bulgur

¹/₂ cup chopped onion (about 1 medium)

4 teaspoons chopped fresh or 1 teaspoon dried sage leaves

4 teaspoons chopped fresh or 1 teaspoon dried marjoram leaves

1 teaspoon salt

¹/₂ teaspoon ground cumin

2 canned chipotle chiles in adobo sauce, finely chopped

1 clove garlic, finely chopped

1 can or bottle (12 ounces) beer or beef broth or Roasted Vegetable Broth (page 15)

2 cups 1-inch cubes peeled buttercup or butternut squash

1 medium red bell pepper, cut into 1-inch pieces

Heat water and beans to boiling in Dutch oven. Boil uncovered 2 minutes; remove from heat. Cover and let stand 1 hour. Heat beans to boiling again; reduce heat. Simmer uncovered 1 hour.

Stir in remaining ingredients except squash and bell pepper. Heat to boiling; reduce heat. Cover and simmer 30 minutes, stirring occasionally. Stir in squash. Cover and simmer 30 minutes, stirring occasionally, until squash is tender. Stir in bell pepper. Cover and simmer about 5 minutes or until bell pepper is crisp-tender. Serve with sour cream if desired. *4 servings*

NUTRITION INFORMATION PER SERVING

ONE SERVING		PERCENT OF U.S. RDA	
Calories	280	Vitamin A	56%
Protein, g	15	Vitamin C	74%
Carbohydrate, g	67	Calcium	12%
Fat, g	2	Iron	24%
Unsaturated	1		
Saturated	1		
Dietary fiber, g	17		
Cholesterol, mg	0		
Sodium, mg	550		

Curried Stew with Peanut Sauce

2 cups broccoli flowerets

2 cups cauliflowerets

1 cup chopped red bell pepper (about 1 medium)

1 cup chopped onion (about 1 large)

1 tablespoon curry powder

1 teaspoon mustard seed

¹/₂ teaspoon cumin seed

2 cloves garlic, finely chopped

1 serrano chile, seeded and finely chopped

3 tablespoons margarine or butter

1 can (14¹/₂ ounces) ready-to-serve chicken broth or 1³/₄ cups Vegetable Broth (page 14)

1 can (15 to 16 ounces) kidney beans, rinsed and drained

²/₃ cups raisins

1 tablespoon lemon juice

3 cups hot cooked rice

Peanut Sauce (right)

Cook broccoli, cauliflowerets, bell pepper, onion, curry powder, mustard seed, cumin seed, garlic and chile in margarine in Dutch oven over me- dium heat about 5 minutes, stirring occasionally, until vegetables are crisp-tender. Stir in broth, beans, raisins and lemon juice. Heat to boiling; reduce heat. Cover and simmer 15 minutes. Serve with rice and Peanut Sauce. Garnish with chopped peanuts and coconut if desired. *6 servings*

PEANUT SAUCE

²/₃ cup vanilla low-fat or regular yogurt

¹/₄ cup creamy peanut butter

¹/₄ cup coconut milk

1 tablespoon soy sauce

¹/₄ to ¹/₂ teaspoon red pepper sauce

Mix all ingredients, using wire whisk.

NUTRITION INFORMATION PER SERVING

ONE SERVING		PERCENT OF U.S. RDA	
Calories	465	Vitamin A	26%
Protein, g	17	Vitamin C	78%
Carbohydrate, g	75	Calcium	12%
Fat, g	15	Iron	30%
Unsaturated	10		
Saturated	5		
Dietary fiber, g	10		
Cholesterol, mg	0		
Sodium, mg	1110		

Vegetable Stew with Dill Dumplings

¹/₂ cup chopped onion (about 1 medium)

1 tablespoon margarine or butter

2 cups cooked dried navy beans

¹/₂ cup uncooked rosamarina (orzo) pasta

4 cups chicken broth or Vegetable Broth (page 14)

1 teaspoon ground mustard

1 package (16 ounces) frozen sweet peas, potatoes and carrots, thawed

Dill Dumplings (below)

Cook onion in margarine in Dutch oven over medium-high heat, stirring occasionally, until onion is tender. Stir in remaining ingredients except Dill Dumplings. Heat to boiling; reduce heat. Meanwhile, prepare Dill Dumplings. Gently drop dough by rounded tablespoonfuls onto simmering stew (do not drop directly into liquid). Cook uncovered over low heat 10 minutes. Cover and cook 10 minutes longer. *4 servings*

DILL DUMPLINGS

1¹/₃ cups Bisquick® baking mix

²/₃ cup cornmeal

2 tablespoons chopped fresh or 2 teaspoons dried dill weed

²/₃ cup milk

Mix baking mix, cornmeal and dill weed. Stir in milk just until dry ingredients are moistened.

NUTRITION INFORMATION PER SERVING

ONE SERVING		PERCENT OF U.S. RDA	
Calories	568	Vitamin A	12%
Protein, g	25	Vitamin C	10%
Carbohydrate, g	103	Calcium	22%
Fat, g	12	Iron	38%
Unsaturated	9		
Saturated	3		
Dietary fiber, g	13		
Cholesterol, mg	5		
Sodium, mg	1450		

Caribbean Stew with Pineapple Salsa

Plantains are a large, firm variety of banana. They are used extensively in Latin America as a main dish staple, not only as a fruit or dessert as in America. A ripe plantain won't be as soft as a ripe banana, but it shouldn't be too hard. If plantains are unavailable, sweet potatoes make a nice substitute.

Pineapple Salsa (right)

1 cup chopped onion (about 1 large)

1 teaspoon chopped gingerroot or 1/4 teaspoon ground ginger

2 cloves garlic, finely chopped

1 tablespoon vegetable oil

2 1/2 cups pineapple juice

1 tablespoon lime juice

1 cup uncooked regular long grain rice

1/2 to 1 teaspoon crushed red pepper

1/2 teaspoon salt

1/4 teaspoon dried thyme leaves

1/4 teaspoon ground cinnamon

Dash of ground allspice

Dash of ground cloves

1 can (15 ounces) black beans, rinsed and drained

1 large ripe plantain or sweet potato, peeled and cut into 1/2-inch pieces

1/3 cup chopped fresh cilantro

Prepare Pineapple Salsa; set aside. Cook onion, gingerroot and garlic in oil in 3-quart saucepan over medium-high heat, stirring occasionally, until onion is tender.

Stir in pineapple juice and lime juice. Heat to boiling. Stir in remaining ingredients except Pineapple Salsa; reduce heat. Cover and simmer 15 to 20 minutes or until almost all liquid is absorbed. Stir in cilantro. Top each serving with Pineapple Salsa. *4 servings*

PINEAPPLE SALSA

1/2 cup coarsely chopped pineapple

1/4 cup coarsely chopped tomatillos or roma (plum) tomatoes

1 tablespoon chopped red bell pepper

1 tablespoon chopped red onion

1/4 teaspoon grated lime peel

1 tablespoon lime juice

Mix all ingredients.

NUTRITION INFORMATION PER SERVING

ONE SERVING		PERCENT OF U.S. RDA	
Calories	550	Vitamin A	12%
Protein, g	15	Vitamin C	38%
Carbohydrate, g	122	Calcium	14%
Fat, g	5	Iron	32%
Unsaturated	4		
Saturated	1		
Dietary fiber, g	11		
Cholesterol, mg	0		
Sodium, mg	530		

Garden Vegetable Stew

³/₄ cup chopped onions (about 1¹/₂ medium)

1 cup thinly sliced carrots (about 2 medium)

2 tablespoons margarine or butter

2 cans (14¹/₂ ounces each) ready-to-serve chicken broth or 3¹/₂ cups Vegetable Broth (page 14)

²/₃ cup uncooked brown rice or regular long grain rice

1 cup fresh or frozen whole kernel corn

1 cup thinly sliced zucchini (about ¹/₂ medium)

1 cup thinly sliced yellow squash (about ¹/₂ medium)

1 tablespoon chopped fresh or 1 teaspoon dried basil leaves

1 teaspoon chopped fresh or ¹/₄ teaspoon dried thyme leaves

¹/₄ teaspoon pepper

1 can (15 to 16 ounces) garbanzo beans, rinsed and drained

1 large red bell pepper, cut into 2×¹/₂-inch strips

4 new potatoes, cut into fourths

Cook onions and carrots in margarine in Dutch oven, stirring occasionally, until onion is tender. Stir in broth and rice. Heat to boiling; reduce heat. Cover and simmer 20 minutes. Stir in remaining ingredients. Cover and simmer 10 to 15 minutes or until vegetables are tender. *4 servings*

NUTRITION INFORMATION PER SERVING

ONE SERVING		PERCENT OF U.S. RDA	
Calories	505	Vitamin A	34%
Protein, g	21	Vitamin C	60%
Carbohydrate, g	93	Calcium	12%
Fat, g	11	Iron	34%
Unsaturated	9		
Saturated	2		
Dietary fiber, g	13		
Cholesterol, mg	0		
Sodium, mg	1010		

Three-Bean Chile

1 cup chopped onion (about 1 large)

2 cloves garlic, crushed

1 can (14¹/₂ ounces) ready-to-serve chicken broth or 1³/₄ cups Vegetable Broth (page 14)

2 cups cubed seeded tomatoes (about 2 large)

2 tablespoons chopped fresh cilantro

1 tablespoon chopped fresh or 1 teaspoon dried oregano leaves

2 teaspoons chile powder

1 teaspoon ground cumin

1 can (15 to 16 ounces) kidney beans, undrained

1 can (15 ounces) spicy chile beans, undrained

1 can (15 to 16 ounces) garbanzo beans, undrained

Cook onion and garlic in ¹/₄ cup of the broth in nonstick Dutch oven over medium heat about 5 minutes, stirring occasionally, until onion is crisp-tender. Stir in remaining broth and remaining ingredients except beans.

Heat to boiling; reduce heat. Cover and simmer 30 minutes, stirring occasionally.

Stir in beans. Heat to boiling; reduce heat. Simmer uncovered 20 minutes, stirring occasionally, until of desired consistency. *5 servings*

NUTRITION INFORMATION PER SERVING

ONE SERVING		PERCENT OF U.S. RDA	
Calories	245	Vitamin A	14%
Protein, g	17	Vitamin C	50%
Carbohydrate, g	53	Calcium	10%
Fat, g	3	Iron	36%
Unsaturated	2		
Saturated	1		
Dietary fiber, g	15		
Cholesterol, mg	0		
Sodium, mg	740		

Tex-Mex Chile

1 cup chopped onion (about 1 large)

¹/₂ cup chopped green bell pepper (about 1 small)

2 cloves garlic, finely chopped

1 tablespoon vegetable oil

2 cups frozen corn with red and green peppers (about 1¹/₄ cups)

2 teaspoons chile powder

1 teaspoon ground cumin

¹/₂ teaspoon dried oregano leaves, crumbled

4 frozen soybean-based vegetable burgers, thawed and cubed

1 can (15 to 16 ounces) kidney beans, rinsed and drained

1 can (15 ounces) no-salt-added or regular tomato sauce

1 jar (10 ounces) thick and chunky salsa

¹/₄ cup sour cream

¹/₄ cup shredded Monterey Jack cheese with jalapeño chiles (1 ounce)

Cook onion, bell pepper and garlic in oil in Dutch oven, stirring occasionally, until onion is tender. Stir in remaining ingredients except sour cream and cheese. Cover and simmer over low heat 30 minutes, stirring occasionally. Top each serving with sour cream and cheese. *4 servings*

NUTRITION INFORMATION PER SERVING

ONE SERVING		PERCENT OF U.S. RDA	
Calories	425	Vitamin A	30%
Protein, g	28	Vitamin C	50%
Carbohydrate, g	50	Calcium	24%
Fat, g	14	Iron	40%
Unsaturated	10		
Saturated	4		
Dietary fiber, g	3		
Cholesterol, mg	10		
Sodium, mg	775		

Chunky Vegetable Chile

2 cups cubed potatoes (about 2 medium)

1/2 cup chopped onion (about 1 medium)

1/2 cup chopped yellow bell pepper (about 1 small)

1 tablespoon chile powder

1 teaspoon ground cumin

1 can (28 ounces) whole tomatoes, undrained

1 can (15 to 16 ounces) garbanzo beans, rinsed and drained

1 can (15 ounces) black beans, rinsed and drained

1 can (8 ounces) tomato sauce

1 cup cubed zucchini (about 1 medium)

Sour cream, if desired

Heat remaining ingredients except zucchini to boiling in Dutch oven, breaking up tomatoes and stirring occasionally; reduce heat. Cover and simmer 13 minutes. Stir in zucchini. Cover and simmer 5 to 7 minutes or until zucchini is tender. Serve with sour cream. *4 servings*

NUTRITION INFORMATION PER SERVING

ONE SERVING		PERCENT OF U.S. RDA	
Calories	420	Vitamin A	36%
Protein, g	23	Vitamin C	68%
Carbohydrate, g	90	Calcium	22%
Fat, g	5	Iron	48%
Unsaturated	4		
Saturated	1		
Dietary fiber, g	20		
Cholesterol, mg	0		
Sodium, mg	1200		

Bean and Pepper Chile

1 to 2 tablespoons chile powder

2 teaspoons ground cumin

1/4 teaspoon pepper

1 can (28 ounces) whole tomatoes, undrained

1 can (15 to 16 ounces) garbanzo beans, rinsed and drained

1 can (15 to 16 ounces) kidney beans, rinsed and drained

1 can (15 to 16 ounces) butter beans, rinsed and drained

1 can (15 ounces) tomato sauce

1 small red bell pepper, cut into 1-inch pieces

1 small green bell pepper, cut into 1-inch pieces

1 small yellow or orange bell pepper, cut into 1-inch pieces

1 Anaheim or jalapeño chile, seeded and chopped

1/2 cup sour cream

3 tablespoons salsa

Mix all ingredients except sour cream and salsa in Dutch oven. Heat to boiling, breaking up tomatoes. Cover and simmer 15 to 20 minutes or until bell peppers are tender. Mix sour cream and salsa. Serve chile with sour cream mixture. *6 servings*

NUTRITION INFORMATION PER SERVING

ONE SERVING		PERCENT OF U.S. RDA	
Calories	260	Vitamin A	26%
Protein, g	15	Vitamin C	50%
Carbohydrate, g	49	Calcium	12%
Fat, g	6	Iron	34%
Unsaturated	3		
Saturated	3		
Dietary fiber, g	13		
Cholesterol, mg	10		
Sodium, mg	1090		

Baked Chile in Polenta Crust

Polenta, or cornmeal mush, makes a unique crust for this temptingly spiced chile.

Polenta Crust (right)
1/2 cup chopped onion (about 1 medium)
1 clove garlic, finely chopped
1 teaspoon vegetable oil
1 tablespoon chile powder
1 teaspoon ground cumin
1/4 teaspoon ground cinnamon
1/4 teaspoon pepper
1 can (15 ounces) tomato sauce
1 can (6 ounces) tomato paste
1 can (15 ounces) black beans, rinsed and drained
1 can (15 to 16 ounces) pinto beans, rinsed and drained
1/2 cup shredded sharp Cheddar cheese (2 ounces)

Prepare Polenta Crust. Heat oven to 350°. Grease 2-quart casserole. Cook onion and garlic in oil in 2-quart saucepan over medium heat about 5 minutes, stirring occasionally, until onion is crisp-tender. Stir in remaining ingredients except cheese. Heat to boiling, stirring occasionally.

Spread or press Polenta Crust mixture on bottom and up side of casserole to form crust. Spoon chile mixture into crust. Bake 30 to 35 minutes or until hot. Sprinkle with cheese. Bake 2 to 3 minutes or until cheese is melted. 6 servings

POLENTA CRUST

1 cup yellow cornmeal
3/4 cup milk
3 1/4 cups boiling water
1 teaspoon salt
3 tablespoons canned chopped green chiles

Mix cornmeal and milk in 2-quart saucepan. Stir in boiling water and salt. Cook, stirring constantly, until mixture thickens and boils; reduce heat. Cover and simmer 10 minutes, stirring occasionally; remove from heat. Stir in chiles. Cool 30 minutes.

NUTRITION INFORMATION PER SERVING

ONE SERVING		PERCENT OF U.S. RDA	
Calories	305	Vitamin A	22%
Protein, g	16	Vitamin C	40%
Carbohydrate, g	58	Calcium	18%
Fat, g	6	Iron	30%
Unsaturated	3		
Saturated	3		
Dietary fiber, g	11		
Cholesterol, mg	10		
Sodium, mg	1370		

Cincinnati Chile

1 large onion, halved and sliced

2 cloves garlic, finely chopped

2 teaspoons vegetable oil

1 cup water

1 tablespoon plus 1 teaspoon chile powder

1 tablespoon cocoa

1 tablespoon chopped fresh or 1 teaspoon
   dried oregano leaves, crumbled

1¼ teaspoons ground cumin

¼ teaspoon ground cinnamon

¼ teaspoon ground coriander

¼ teaspoon pepper

2 cans (15 to 16 ounces each) kidney
   beans, rinsed and drained

1 can (15 ounces) tomato sauce

1 can (6 ounces) tomato paste

2 cups hot cooked spaghetti

½ cup shredded Cheddar cheese (2
   ounces)

¼ cup chopped onion (about 1 small)

Corn chips or oyster crackers, if desired

Cook sliced onion and garlic in oil in 3-quart saucepan over medium heat about 5 minutes, stirring occasionally, until onion is crisp-tender. Stir in remaining ingredients except spaghetti, cheese, chopped onion and corn chips. Heat to boiling; reduce heat. Cover and simmer 30 minutes. Place ½ cup spaghetti in each of 4 soup bowls. Ladle chile over spaghetti. Serve with cheese, chopped onion and corn chips. *4 servings*

NUTRITION INFORMATION PER SERVING

ONE SERVING		PERCENT OF U.S. RDA	
Calories	420	Vitamin A	32%
Protein, g	24	Vitamin C	50%
Carbohydrate, g	76	Calcium	18%
Fat, g	10	Iron	48%
Unsaturated	6		
Saturated	4		
Dietary fiber, g	18		
Cholesterol, mg	15		
Sodium, mg	1540		

Green Jerked Chile

"Jerk" refers to a blend of seasonings popular among the islands of the Caribbean. While ingredients vary from island to island, thyme, allspice and lime predominate in the seasoning mixture.

1 cup chopped green onions (about 10 medium)

1 medium green bell pepper, cut into 2×¼-inch strips

1 to 2 jalapeño chiles, seeded and chopped

1 clove garlic, finely chopped

1 tablespoon margarine or butter

¼ cup chopped fresh cilantro

3 cups chicken broth or Vegetable Broth (page 14)

1 tablespoon chopped fresh or 1 teaspoon dried thyme leaves

1 tablespoon lime juice

1 teaspoon grated lime peel

1 teaspoon chile powder

¼ teaspoon ground cinnamon

¼ teaspoon ground allspice

1 can (15 to 16 ounces) kidney beans, rinsed and drained

1 can (15 to 16 ounces) great northern beans, rinsed and drained

Cook onions, bell pepper, chiles and garlic in margarine in 3-quart saucepan over medium heat about 5 minutes, stirring occasionally, until vegetables are crisp-tender. Stir in remaining ingredients. Heat to boiling; reduce heat. Cover and simmer 20 minutes. *4 servings*

NUTRITION INFORMATION PER SERVING

ONE SERVING		PERCENT OF U.S. RDA	
Calories	240	Vitamin A	22%
Protein, g	18	Vitamin C	50%
Carbohydrate, g	43	Calcium	14%
Fat, g	5	Iron	38%
Unsaturated	4		
Saturated	1		
Dietary fiber, g	12		
Cholesterol, mg	0		
Sodium, mg	980		

Three-Bean White Chile

Tomatillo Salsa (right)

1 cup chopped onion (about 1 large)

1 cup chopped yellow bell pepper (about 1 medium)

2 jalapeño chiles, seeded and chopped

2 cloves garlic, finely chopped

¼ cup (½ stick) margarine or butter

3 cups water

2 tablespoons lime juice

1 teaspoon grated lime peel

1 teaspoon cumin seed

½ teaspoon dried oregano leaves

½ teaspoon ground coriander

¼ teaspoon salt

1 can (15 to 16 ounces) great northern beans, rinsed and drained

1 can (15 to 16 ounces) butter beans, rinsed and drained

1 can (15 to 16 ounces) black-eyed peas, rinsed and drained

Prepare Tomatillo Salsa. Cook onion, bell pepper, chiles and garlic in margarine in Dutch oven, stirring occasionally, until onion is tender. Stir in remaining ingredients. Heat to boiling; reduce heat. Simmer uncovered 20 minutes. Serve with salsa. *6 servings*

TOMATILLO SALSA

¼ cup chopped green onions (2 to 3 medium)

¼ cup chopped fresh cilantro

2 tablespoons pine nuts, toasted

1 tablespoon lime juice

¼ teaspoon salt

½ pound tomatillos or roma (plum) tomatoes or green tomatoes, chopped

1 jalapeño chile, seeded and chopped

Mix all ingredients. Cover and refrigerate 30 minutes to blend flavors.

NUTRITION INFORMATION PER SERVING

ONE SERVING		PERCENT OF U.S. RDA	
Calories	320	Vitamin A	42%
Protein, g	20	Vitamin C	68%
Carbohydrate, g	56	Calcium	12%
Fat, g	10	Iron	40%
Unsaturated	8		
Saturated	2		
Dietary fiber, g	18		
Cholesterol, mg	0		
Sodium, mg	790		

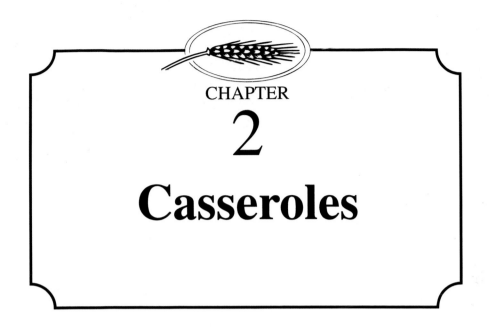

CHAPTER

2

Casseroles

C asseroles are the mainstays of busy people, combining ease of preparation with no-fuss cooking. These meatless casseroles are inventive and delicious; try Southwest Vegetable Stew with Cornbread Topping, Baked Risotto, Phyllo and Spinach Pie, or an elegant Pasta Torte. You'll be pleasantly surprised at how satisfying these casseroles without meat can be, and how enticing!

Anasazi Enchiladas (page 34)

Black Bean-Tortilla Pie

½ cup chopped onion (about 1 medium)

½ cup chopped seeded tomato (about 1 small)

1 small jalapeño chile, seeded and finely chopped

1 can (11 ounces) tomatillos, drained

1 tablespoon vegetable oil

1 can (15 ounces) black beans, drained and 3 tablespoons liquid reserved

½ cup chopped red bell pepper (about 1 small)

¼ cup chopped green onions (2 to 3 medium)

1 teaspoon ground cumin

1 egg

1 egg white

1 can (15 ounces) black beans, rinsed and drained

8 corn tortillas (6 inches in diameter)

½ cup shredded reduced-fat or regular Monterey Jack cheese (2 ounces)

1½ cups salsa

¾ cup plain nonfat or regular yogurt

Heat oven to 375°. Grease 3-quart casserole. Place onion, tomato, chile and tomatillos in blender or food processor. Cover and blend or process until smooth. Cook tomatillo sauce and oil in 12-inch skillet over medium heat 3 minutes, stirring occasionally.

Place 1 can black beans and 3 tablespoons bean liquid in blender or food processor. Cover and blend just until chunky. Mix chunky beans, bell pepper, green onions and cumin in large bowl. Stir in egg, egg white and remaining black beans.

Place 2 tortillas in casserole. Layer with 1 cup bean mixture, 2 tortillas, ½ cup tomatillo sauce, 2 tortillas, remaining bean mixture, 2 tortillas, remaining tomatillo sauce and cheese. Bake uncovered about 35 minutes or until cheese is melted. Let stand 5 minutes before serving. Serve with salsa and yogurt. *6 servings*

NUTRITION INFORMATION PER SERVING

ONE SERVING		PERCENT OF U.S. RDA	
Calories	390	Vitamin A	24%
Protein, g	23	Vitamin C	28%
Carbohydrate, g	70	Calcium	36%
Fat, g	8	Iron	32%
Unsaturated	6		
Saturated	2		
Dietary fiber, g	14		
Cholesterol, mg	40		
Sodium, mg	1220		

Red Beans and Rice

Try this southern classic with split and toasted cornbread squares.

*1 cup chopped celery (**about 2 medium stalks**)*

*1 cup chopped onion (**about 1 large**)*

*³/₄ cup chopped green bell pepper (**about 1 medium**)*

1 clove garlic, finely chopped

1 tablespoon vegetable oil

1¹/₂ cups uncooked regular long grain rice

*2 cups peeled cubed cooked acorn, buttercup or butternut squash (**about 1 medium**)*

*6 cups Roasted Vegetable Broth (**page 15**) or water*

1 tablespoon chopped fresh or 1 teaspoon dried thyme leaves

2 teaspoons chopped fresh or ¹/₂ teaspoon dried oregano leaves

¹/₂ teaspoon salt

¹/₂ teaspoon white pepper

¹/₄ to ¹/₂ teaspoon red pepper sauce

*1 can (**15 to 16 ounces**) kidney beans, rinsed and drained*

Heat oven to 375°. Grease 3-quart casserole. Cook celery, onion, bell pepper and garlic in oil in 12-inch skillet, stirring occasionally, until vegetables are crisp-tender. Stir in rice. Cook 3 minutes, stirring frequently, until rice is coated with oil. Stir in remaining ingredients; spoon into casserole. Cover and bake about 50 minutes or until rice is tender and liquid is absorbed. Let stand 5 minutes before serving. *6 servings*

NUTRITION INFORMATION PER SERVING

ONE SERVING		PERCENT OF U.S. RDA	
Calories	310	Vitamin A	30%
Protein, g	11	Vitamin C	18%
Carbohydrate, g	68	Calcium	6%
Fat, g	4	Iron	24%
Unsaturated	3		
Saturated	1		
Dietary fiber, g	10		
Cholesterol, mg	0		
Sodium, mg	370		

Anasazi Enchiladas

1 can (16 ounces) whole tomatoes, undrained

1/2 cup chopped onion (about 1 medium)

1 clove garlic, finely chopped

1/4 cup chopped fresh cilantro

2 teaspoons honey

1/8 teaspoon crushed red pepper

2 cups cooked dried Anasazi or pinto beans or 1 can (15 to 16 ounces) pinto beans, rinsed and drained

1 cup low-fat or regular ricotta cheese

1/2 cup chopped green bell pepper (about 1 small)

1 teaspoon ground cumin

6 flour tortillas (8 inches in diameter)

1/4 cup shredded Cheddar cheese (1 ounce)

1/4 cup shredded Monterey Jack cheese (1 ounce)

Heat oven to 375°. Grease rectangular baking dish, 11×7×1½ inches. Place tomatoes, onion and garlic in blender or food processor. Cover and blend or process until smooth. Cook blended mixture, 2 tablespoons of the cilantro, the honey and red pepper in 2-quart saucepan over medium heat 3 minutes, stirring occasionally.

Mix together beans, ricotta cheese, bell pepper, cumin and remaining cilantro. Spread ½ cup tomato sauce in baking dish. Spoon ½ cup bean mixture on one side of each tortilla. Roll up tortilla; place seam side down on tomato sauce in baking dish. Spoon remaining tomato sauce over filled tortillas. Sprinkle with cheeses. Bake 20 to 25 minutes or until tomato sauce is bubbly and cheese is melted. *6 servings*

NUTRITION INFORMATION PER SERVING

ONE SERVING		PERCENT OF U.S. RDA	
Calories	320	Vitamin A	12%
Protein, g	16	Vitamin C	20%
Carbohydrate, g	47	Calcium	24%
Fat, g	10	Iron	24%
Unsaturated	5		
Saturated	5		
Dietary fiber, g	6		
Cholesterol, mg	25		
Sodium, mg	400		

Southern Peas and Greens

2 cups milk

2 tablespoons all-purpose flour

2 tablespoons honey

2 tablespoons lemon juice

1 teaspoon salt

1/2 teaspoon pepper

1/2 teaspoon ground nutmeg

1/4 cup nonfat cream cheese product or regular cream cheese, softened

2 cups hot cooked elbow lupini pasta or elbow macaroni

2 cups cooked chopped mustard greens, collard greens or spinach (about 1 large bunch)

1 cup chopped green bell pepper (about 1 medium)

1 cup chopped leeks with tops (about 2 medium)

1 can (15 to 16 ounces) black-eyed peas, rinsed and drained

1/4 cup soft whole wheat or white bread crumbs

Heat oven to 375°. Grease 3-quart casserole. Mix milk and flour in 1-quart saucepan. Heat to boiling, stirring constantly. Boil and stir 1 minute; remove from heat. Stir in honey, lemon juice, salt, pepper, nutmeg and cream cheese. Pour sauce into large bowl. Stir in remaining ingredients except bread crumbs; spoon into casserole. Sprinkle with bread crumbs. Bake uncovered about 35 minutes or until golden brown. *6 servings*

NUTRITION INFORMATION PER SERVING

ONE SERVING		PERCENT OF U.S. RDA	
Calories	275	Vitamin A	56%
Protein, g	15	Vitamin C	36%
Carbohydrate, g	48	Calcium	26%
Fat, g	3	Iron	18%
Unsaturated	2		
Saturated	1		
Dietary fiber, g	1		
Cholesterol, mg	10		
Sodium, mg	580		

Zucchini-Pinto Casserole

3 tablespoons all-purpose flour

1 teaspoon salt

¹/₂ teaspoon pepper

2¹/₂ cups milk

6 cups sliced zucchini (about 1¹/₂ pounds)

1 can (8 ounces) tomato sauce

1 can (15 to 16 ounces) pinto beans, rinsed and drained

1¹/₂ cups soft whole wheat or white bread crumbs

2 tablespoons shredded part-skim or regular mozzarella cheese

3 egg whites

Heat oven to 375°. Grease 3-quart casserole. Mix flour, salt, pepper and milk in 2-quart saucepan. Heat to boiling, stirring constantly. Boil and stir 1 minute. Stir in zucchini, tomato sauce and beans; spoon into casserole. Mix bread crumbs, cheese and egg whites; spread over zucchini mixture. Bake uncovered about 40 minutes or until golden brown and bubbly. *6 servings*

NUTRITION INFORMATION PER SERVING

ONE SERVING		PERCENT OF U.S. RDA	
Calories	290	Vitamin A	14%
Protein, g	17	Vitamin C	16%
Carbohydrate, g	54	Calcium	24%
Fat, g	4	Iron	22%
Unsaturated	2		
Saturated	2		
Dietary fiber, g	8		
Cholesterol, mg	10		
Sodium, mg	1060		

Mixed Pepper and Bean Chile

1 cup chopped onion (about 1 large)

1 cup tomato juice

1 tablespoon chile powder

1 teaspoon ground cinnamon

¼ teaspoon pepper

1 clove garlic, finely chopped

4 cups cooked brown rice

2 cups dried kidney beans, cooked, or 1 can (15 to 16 ounces) kidney beans, rinsed and drained

2 cups dried black beans, cooked, or 1 can (15 ounces) black beans, rinsed and drained

1 cup chopped red bell pepper (about 1 medium)

½ cup chopped green bell pepper (about 1 small)

2 cups unsweetened apple juice or water

1 jalapeño chile, seeded and finely chopped

⅓ cup sunflower nuts

1 cup plain nonfat or regular yogurt

¾ cup shredded white Cheddar cheese (3 ounces)

Heat oven to 350°. Grease 3-quart casserole. Heat onion, tomato juice, chile powder, cinnamon, pepper and garlic to boiling in 3-quart saucepan over medium-high heat, stirring occasionally; reduce heat to medium-low. Cook about 5 minutes or until liquid has evaporated; remove from heat. Stir in remaining ingredients except nuts, yogurt and cheese.

Spoon mixture into casserole. Sprinkle with nuts. Bake uncovered 1 hour or until chile is bubbly and nuts are brown. Serve with yogurt and cheese. *6 servings*

NUTRITION INFORMATION PER SERVING

ONE SERVING		PERCENT OF U.S. RDA	
Calories	460	Vitamin A	20%
Protein, g	22	Vitamin C	46%
Carbohydrate, g	81	Calcium	26%
Fat, g	11	Iron	30%
Unsaturated	7		
Saturated	4		
Dietary fiber, g	13		
Cholesterol, mg	15		
Sodium, mg	730		

Southwest Vegetable Stew with Corn Bread Topping

¾ cup chopped onion (about 1 large)

2 Anaheim chiles, seeded and chopped

1 clove garlic, crushed

1 tablespoon vegetable oil

2 cups sliced yellow squash (about 2 medium)

1 cup Roasted Vegetable Broth (page 15) or chicken broth

2 cans (15 to 16 ounces each) pinto beans, rinsed and drained

1 can (17 ounces) whole kernel corn, drained

Corn Bread Topping (right)

8 bell pepper slices

Heat oven to 425°. Cook onion, chiles and garlic in oil in 3-quart saucepan over medium heat about 4 minutes, stirring occasionally, until onion is crisp-tender. Stir in squash, Roasted Vegetable Broth, beans and corn. Cook uncovered about 10 minutes, stirring occasionally, until squash is tender; spoon into 3-quart ungreased casserole.

Prepare Corn Bread Topping. Pour topping over vegetable mixture; carefully spread to cover, sealing to edge of casserole. Arrange bell pepper slices on topping. Bake uncovered 15 to 20 minutes or until topping is golden brown. *6 servings*

CORN BREAD TOPPING

1 1/2 cups yellow cornmeal

1 cup nonfat or regular sour cream

1/2 cup all-purpose flour

2/3 cup milk

1/4 cup vegetable oil

2 teaspoons baking powder

1/2 teaspoon baking soda

1/4 teaspoon salt

1 egg

Mix all ingredients; beat vigorously 30 seconds.

NUTRITION INFORMATION PER SERVING

ONE SERVING		PERCENT OF U.S. RDA	
Calories	485	Vitamin A	30%
Protein, g	18	Vitamin C	52%
Carbohydrate, g	78	Calcium	22%
Fat, g	15	Iron	28%
Unsaturated	10		
Saturated	5		
Dietary fiber, g	9		
Cholesterol, mg	50		
Sodium, mg	820		

Indian Mixed Beans and Rice

5 cups water

1 cup dried whole green mung beans

2 teaspoons curry powder

1 teaspoon ground ginger

1/2 teaspoon ground cinnamon

2 cups shredded red cabbage (about 1/2 pound)

1 cup chopped red onion (about 1 medium)

1 cup apple juice

1 tablespoon vegetable oil

3 cups hot cooked regular long grain rice

1/4 cup currants

1 teaspoon salt

1/2 teaspoon pepper

1/2 package (8-ounce size) light cream cheese (Neufchâtel) or regular cream cheese, softened and cut into 1/2-inch pieces

1 can (15 to 16 ounces) garbanzo beans, rinsed and drained

1 1/2 cups vanilla nonfat or regular yogurt

Heat water and mung beans to boiling in 3-quart saucepan. Boil uncovered 2 minutes; remove from heat. Cover and let stand 1 hour.

Heat mung beans and water to boiling again, stirring occasionally; reduce heat to medium-low. Stir in curry powder, ginger and cinnamon. Cook 20 to 30 minutes, stirring occasionally, until beans are tender.

Meanwhile, heat oven to 375°. Grease 3-quart casserole. Cook cabbage, onion, apple juice and oil in 12-inch nonstick skillet over medium heat 5 to 7 minutes, stirring occasionally, until cabbage softens and liquid evaporates. Drain mung beans, and return to saucepan. Stir in cabbage mixture and remaining ingredients except yogurt. Spoon mixture into casserole. Bake uncovered 25 to 30 minutes or until golden brown. Serve with yogurt.
6 servings

NUTRITION INFORMATION PER SERVING

ONE SERVING		PERCENT OF U.S. RDA	
Calories	495	Vitamin A	8%
Protein, g	22	Vitamin C	12%
Carbohydrate, g	91	Calcium	26%
Fat, g	9	Iron	42%
Unsaturated	6		
Saturated	3		
Dietary fiber, g	10		
Cholesterol, mg	10		
Sodium, mg	1060		

Baked Lentils with Tarragon Rice

3 cups hot cooked regular long grain rice

2 cups frozen green peas

1³/₄ cups hot cooked lentils

1 cup chopped green onions (about 10 medium)

1 tablespoon chopped fresh or 1 teaspoon dried tarragon leaves

1 teaspoon salt

¹/₂ teaspoon pepper

1 package (10 ounces) frozen chopped spinach, thawed and drained

¹/₄ cup soft whole wheat or white bread crumbs

¹/₄ cup ¹/₂-inch pieces reduced-fat or regular Monterey Jack cheese

Heat oven to 350°. Grease 3-quart casserole. Mix all ingredients except bread crumbs and cheese; spoon into casserole. Top with bread crumbs and cheese. Bake uncovered about 35 minutes or until cheese is golden brown. *6 servings*

NUTRITION INFORMATION PER SERVING

ONE SERVING		PERCENT OF U.S. RDA	
Calories	255	Vitamin A	28%
Protein, g	13	Vitamin C	10%
Carbohydrate, g	53	Calcium	12%
Fat, g	2	Iron	26%
Unsaturated	1		
Saturated	1		
Dietary fiber, g	5		
Cholesterol, mg	7		
Sodium, mg	880		

Lentil Loaf

This hearty loaf is similar in texture to meatloaf and can be served with salsa, ketchup or a light cucumber-yogurt sauce. To boost the protein here, serve with rice, pasta or potatoes.

1 cup finely chopped onion (about 1 large)

1 clove garlic, crushed

1 teaspoon olive or vegetable oil

1 cup cooked lentils

1 cup finely chopped tomato (about 1 large)

³/₄ cup dry bread crumbs

¹/₄ cup chopped fresh parsley

¹/₂ teaspoon salt

¹/₂ teaspoon ground cumin

1 egg plus 1 egg white

Heat oven to 350°. Grease loaf pan, 8¹/₂×4¹/₂×2¹/₂ inches. Cook onion and garlic in oil in 10-inch skillet over medium heat about 2 minutes, stirring occasionally, until onion is crisp-tender. Mix onion mixture and remaining ingredients; spoon into loaf pan. Bake uncovered 30 to 40 minutes or until golden brown. Let stand 5 minutes before removing from pan. Serve with salsa or ketchup if desired. *6 servings*

NUTRITION INFORMATION PER SERVING

ONE SERVING		PERCENT OF U.S. RDA	
Calories	110	Vitamin A	4%
Protein, g	6	Vitamin C	8%
Carbohydrate, g	20	Calcium	4%
Fat, g	2	Iron	12%
Unsaturated	1		
Saturated	1		
Dietary fiber, g	3		
Cholesterol, mg	35		
Sodium, mg	340		

Lentil Loaf

Baked Polenta Supper

4 cups milk

2 cups water

1½ cups yellow cornmeal

4 ounces nonfat cream cheese product or regular cream cheese, softened

1 can (15 ounces) tomato sauce

2 egg whites

1 can (14 ounces) artichoke hearts, drained and cut into fourths

1 cup low-fat or regular ricotta cheese

¼ cup shredded part-skim mozzarella cheese (1 ounce)

1 tablespoon grated Parmesan cheese

Heat oven to 375°. Grease rectangular baking dish, 11×7×1½ inches. Cook milk, water and cornmeal in 3-quart saucepan over medium heat 12 to 15 minutes, stirring occasionally, until mixture begins to pull away from side of saucepan; remove from heat. Stir in cream cheese product. Pour into baking dish; cool 15 minutes.

Meanwhile, grease 3-quart casserole. Beat tomato sauce and egg whites in bowl, using wire whisk. Stir in artichoke hearts. Cut cooled cornmeal mixture into 6 squares. Place 3 squares in casserole. Layer with ricotta cheese, artichoke mixture and remaining 3 squares cornmeal mixture. Cover and bake about 25 minutes or until bubbly. Sprinkle with mozzarella and Parmesan cheeses. Bake uncovered about 10 minutes or until cheese is melted. *6 servings*

NUTRITION INFORMATION PER SERVING

ONE SERVING		PERCENT OF U.S. RDA	
Calories	365	Vitamin A	26%
Protein, g	20	Vitamin C	12%
Carbohydrate, g	48	Calcium	40%
Fat, g	12	Iron	16%
Unsaturated	5		
Saturated	7		
Dietary fiber, g	4		
Cholesterol, mg	40		
Sodium, mg	770		

Polenta with Cheese

Additional protein can be added to this polenta by substituting milk for the water. You can also top it with seasoned black beans or kidney beans and chopped fresh vegetables.

1 cup yellow cornmeal

¾ cup water

3¼ cups boiling water

2 teaspoons salt

1 tablespoon margarine or butter

1 cup grated Parmesan cheese

⅓ cup shredded Swiss or Kashkaval cheese

Heat oven to 350°. Grease 1½-quart casserole. Mix cornmeal and ¾ cup water in 2-quart saucepan. Stir in the boiling water and salt. Cook, stirring constantly, until mixture thickens and boils; reduce heat. Cover and simmer 10 minutes, stirring occasionally; remove from heat. Stir until smooth.

Spread one-third of the cornmeal mixture in casserole. Dot with 1 teaspoon of the margarine. Sprinkle with ⅓ cup of the Parmesan cheese. Repeat twice. Sprinkle with Swiss cheese. Bake uncovered 15 to 20 minutes or until hot and bubbly. *6 servings*

NUTRITION INFORMATION PER SERVING

ONE SERVING		PERCENT OF U.S. RDA	
Calories	180	Vitamin A	6%
Protein, g	9	Vitamin C	0%
Carbohydrate, g	19	Calcium	24%
Fat, g	8	Iron	6%
Unsaturated	4		
Saturated	4		
Dietary fiber, g	1		
Cholesterol, mg	15		
Sodium, mg	1000		

Quinoa-Vegetable Bake

6 cups hot cooked quinoa

2 cups cooked 1/4-inch slices zucchini (about 1 medium)

2 cups shredded carrots (about 3 medium)

2 cups finely chopped mushrooms (about 8 ounces)

1 cup chopped celery (about 2 medium stalks)

1 cup low-fat ricotta or regular cheese

1/2 cup frozen whole kernel corn

2 tablespoons pesto

1/4 teaspoon salt

2 egg whites

1/4 cup shredded Havarti or Monterey Jack cheese (1 ounce)

Heat oven to 375°. Grease 3-quart casserole. Mix all ingredients except Havarti cheese; spoon into casserole. Sprinkle with cheese. Bake uncovered 25 to 30 minutes or golden brown. *6 servings*

NUTRITION INFORMATION PER SERVING

ONE SERVING		PERCENT OF U.S. RDA	
Calories	355	Vitamin A	100%
Protein, g	18	Vitamin C	6%
Carbohydrate, g	48	Calcium	22%
Fat, g	11	Iron	32%
Unsaturated	8		
Saturated	3		
Dietary fiber, g	2		
Cholesterol, mg	15		
Sodium, mg	260		

Savory Southwest Loaf

This creamy, slightly chewy grain loaf is excellent served with flour tortillas, a side dish of corn and a variety of salsas.

2 3/4 cups cooked bulgur

1 cup cooked brown or regular long grain rice

1 cup nonfat or regular sour cream

3/4 cup shredded Monterey Jack cheese (3 ounces)

1/2 teaspoon chili powder

2 cans (4 ounces each) chopped green chiles, undrained

Heat oven to 350°. Mix all ingredients in ungreased loaf pan, 9×5×3 inches. Bake uncovered 30 to 35 minutes or until set. *6 servings*

NUTRITION INFORMATION PER SERVING

ONE SERVING		PERCENT OF U.S. RDA	
Calories	235	Vitamin A	12%
Protein, g	9	Vitamin C	32%
Carbohydrate, g	33	Calcium	16%
Fat, g	2	Iron	6%
Unsaturated	4		
Saturated	8		
Dietary fiber, g	6		
Cholesterol, mg	40		
Sodium, mg	1240		

Moussaka

1 medium eggplant (about 1¹/₄ pounds)

¹/₄ cup all-purpose flour

¹/₂ teaspoon salt

¹/₂ teaspoon pepper

¹/₄ teaspoon ground nutmeg

¹/₄ teaspoon ground cinnamon

3 cups milk

4 ounces nonfat cream cheese product or regular cream cheese, softened

4 frozen soybean-based vegetable burgers, thawed and cut into 1-inch pieces

1 can (15 ounces) tomato sauce

¹/₂ cup Egg Substitute (page 88) or cholesterol-free egg product or 2 eggs

Heat oven to 375°. Grease 3-quart casserole. Cut eggplant into ¹/₄-inch slices. Cook eggplant in enough boiling water to cover 5 to 8 minutes or until tender; drain. Mix flour, salt, pepper, nutmeg, cinnamon and milk in 2-quart saucepan. Heat to boiling, stirring constantly. Boil and stir 1 minute; remove from heat. Stir in cream cheese until smooth.

Place half of the eggplant in casserole. Layer with burgers, tomato sauce, 1¹/₂ cups of the white sauce and remaining eggplant. Mix remaining white sauce and Egg Substitute; pour over eggplant. Bake uncovered about 1 hour or until firm. Let stand 10 minutes before serving. *4 servings*

NUTRITION INFORMATION PER SERVING

ONE SERVING		PERCENT OF U.S. RDA	
Calories	375	Vitamin A	50%
Protein, g	33	Vitamin C	40%
Carbohydrate, g	38	Calcium	52%
Fat, g	12	Iron	40%
Unsaturated	8		
Saturated	4		
Dietary fiber, g	4		
Cholesterol, mg	20		
Sodium, mg	1530		

Tabbouleh Casserole

2 cups uncooked bulgur

2 medium onions, thinly sliced

1 cup chopped carrots (about 2 medium)

1 cup chopped fresh pineapple

¹/₂ cup boiling unsweetened apple juice or water

2 tablespoons chopped fresh or 2 teaspoons dried mint leaves

2 tablespoons red wine vinegar or cider vinegar

2 tablespoons honey

1 tablespoon tahini (sesame seed paste)*

1 teaspoon salt

¹/₂ teaspoon pepper

¹/₄ cup shredded Havarti or Monterey Jack cheese (1 ounce)

Heat oven to 375°. Grease 3-quart casserole. Cook bulgur as directed on package—except omit salt. Mix bulgur and remaining ingredients except cheese; spoon into casserole. Sprinkle with cheese. Bake uncovered 20 to 25 minutes or until golden brown. *6 servings*

* Tahini may be purchased at specialty and health food stores, as well as at most grocery stores.

NUTRITION INFORMATION PER SERVING

ONE SERVING		PERCENT OF U.S. RDA	
Calories	310	Vitamin A	28%
Protein, g	11	Vitamin C	6%
Carbohydrate, g	72	Calcium	8%
Fat, g	4	Iron	14%
Unsaturated	2		
Saturated	2		
Dietary fiber, g	15		
Cholesterol, mg	5		
Sodium, mg	2250		

Tabbouleh Casserole, Pizza Pot Pie (page 44)

Pizza Pot Pie

1 cup chopped mushrooms

½ medium red onion, sliced

2 cloves garlic, finely chopped

1 tablespoon vegetable or olive oil

1 cup chopped green bell pepper

1 can (6 ounces) pitted ripe olives, drained and coarsely chopped

1 can (8 ounces) tomato sauce

4 frozen soybean-based vegetable burgers, thawed and cubed

2 cups Bisquick® reduced-fat or regular original baking and pancake mix

⅓ cup milk

1 tablespoon grated Parmesan cheese

1 egg white

Heat oven to 400°. Grease 3-quart casserole. Cook mushrooms, onion and garlic in oil in 12-inch skillet 3 to 5 minutes, stirring occasionally, until mushrooms are soft; remove from heat. Stir in bell pepper, olives and tomato sauce. Stir in burgers; spoon into casserole.

Mix remaining ingredients. Turn dough onto floured surface; gently roll in flour to coat. Knead 5 or 6 times. Pat dough into 9-inch circle; place on mixture in casserole and cut several slits in dough. Bake uncovered 25 to 35 minutes or until golden brown. Let stand 5 minutes before serving. *4 servings*

NUTRITION INFORMATION PER SERVING

ONE SERVING		PERCENT OF U.S. RDA	
Calories	485	Vitamin A	18%
Protein, g	26	Vitamin C	62%
Carbohydrate, g	57	Calcium	26%
Fat, g	19	Iron	44%
Unsaturated	15		
Saturated	4		
Dietary fiber, g	5		
Cholesterol, mg	5		
Sodium, mg	1590		

Baked Risotto

4 cups hot cooked regular long grain rice

4 cups cooked dried lima beans or 2 packages (10 ounces each) frozen lima beans, thawed

1 cup chopped green onions (about 10 medium)

½ cup ½-inch cubes Havarti cheese (about 4 ounces)

2 teaspoons chopped fresh cilantro

1 teaspoon salt

½ teaspoon pepper

¼ cup wheat germ

1 tablespoon grated Parmesan cheese

Heat oven to 350°. Grease 3-quart casserole. Mix all ingredients except wheat germ and Parmesan cheese; spoon into casserole. Sprinkle with wheat germ and Parmesan cheese. Bake uncovered about 45 minutes or until golden brown. *6 servings*

NUTRITION INFORMATION PER SERVING

ONE SERVING		PERCENT OF U.S. RDA	
Calories	335	Vitamin A	4%
Protein, g	15	Vitamin C	16%
Carbohydrate, g	65	Calcium	12%
Fat, g	5	Iron	22%
Unsaturated	2		
Saturated	3		
Dietary fiber, g	8		
Cholesterol, mg	10		
Sodium, mg	1020		

Kasha and Cabbage

10 cups chopped green cabbage

1 cup chopped red onion

1 cup chopped green apple

2 cups apple juice

2 tablespoons red wine vinegar

2 tablespoons honey

1 tablespoon margarine or butter

1 cup uncooked roasted buckwheat kernels (kasha)

1 egg

1 cup chopped fresh parsley

1¹/₄ cups low-fat or regular buttermilk

1¹/₂ cups plain nonfat or regular yogurt

³/₄ cup shredded Gouda cheese

Heat oven to 375°. Grease 3-quart casserole. Heat cabbage, onion, apple, apple juice, vinegar, honey and margarine to boiling in 3-quart saucepan over medium-high heat, stirring occasionally; reduce heat to medium-low. Cook 7 to 10 minutes or until cabbage is wilted. Meanwhile, cook buckwheat kernels and egg in 10-inch nonstick skillet over medium heat 3 minutes, stirring occasionally, until dry.

Remove cabbage mixture from heat; stir in buckwheat mixture, parsley and buttermilk. Spoon mixture into casserole. Cover and bake 30 minutes or until cabbage and buckwheat are tender. Fluff buckwheat mixture with fork. Serve with yogurt and cheese. *6 servings*

NUTRITION INFORMATION PER SERVING

ONE SERVING		PERCENT OF U.S. RDA	
Calories	290	Vitamin A	12%
Protein, g	14	Vitamin C	60%
Carbohydrate, g	48	Calcium	36%
Fat, g	7	Iron	12%
Unsaturated	4		
Saturated	3		
Dietary fiber, g	5		
Cholesterol, mg	45		
Sodium, mg	240		

Baked Orzo and Vegetables

4 cups hot cooked rosamarina (orzo) pasta

1 cup chopped tomato (about 1 large)

1 cup cooked dried garbanzo beans or canned garbanzo beans (rinsed and drained)

2 tablespoons soft whole wheat or white bread crumbs

1 tablespoon grated Parmesan cheese

1 tablespoon pesto

¹/₄ teaspoon pepper

1 clove garlic, finely chopped

3 egg whites

1 egg

1 package (10 ounces) frozen chopped spinach, thawed and drained

Heat oven to 350°. Grease 3-quart casserole. Mix all ingredients; spoon into casserole. Bake uncovered about 30 minutes or until golden brown. *4 servings*

NUTRITION INFORMATION PER SERVING

ONE SERVING		PERCENT OF U.S. RDA	
Calories	335	Vitamin A	42%
Protein, g	18	Vitamin C	12%
Carbohydrate, g	59	Calcium	14%
Fat, g	5	Iron	24%
Unsaturated	4		
Saturated	1		
Dietary fiber, g	5		
Cholesterol, mg	55		
Sodium, mg	380		

Minted Couscous and Red Lentil Pilaf

Red lentils are smaller than brown and green lentils, and they cook more quickly.

6 cups hot cooked couscous

2³/4 cups cooked red lentils

1/2 cup chopped tomato (about 1 small)

1/2 cup raisins

2 tablespoons chopped fresh or 2 teaspoons dried mint leaves

1/4 teaspoon pepper

1/8 teaspoon ground red pepper (cayenne)

1/3 cup crumbled feta cheese

Heat oven to 400°. Grease 3-quart casserole. Mix all ingredients except cheese; spoon into casserole. Cover and bake 20 minutes. Sprinkle with cheese. Bake uncovered about 10 minutes or until cheese is melted. *6 servings*

NUTRITION INFORMATION PER SERVING

ONE SERVING		PERCENT OF U.S. RDA	
Calories	365	Vitamin A	2%
Protein, g	16	Vitamin C	4%
Carbohydrate, g	71	Calcium	6%
Fat, g	2	Iron	22%
Unsaturated	1		
Saturated	1		
Dietary fiber, g	7		
Cholesterol, mg	5		
Sodium, mg	480		

Macaroni and Cheese

1 to 1¹/2 cups uncooked elbow macaroni, rigatoni or spinach egg noodles

1/4 cup chopped onion (about 1 small)

1/2 teaspoon salt

1/4 teaspoon pepper

2 tablespoons margarine or butter

1/4 cup all-purpose flour

1³/4 cups milk

6 ounces process sharp American cheese loaf, cut into 1/2-inch cubes

Heat oven to 375°. Cook macaroni as directed on package; drain. Cook onion, salt and pepper in margarine over medium heat, stirring occasionally, until onion is crisp-tender. Mix flour and milk until smooth. Stir into onion mixture. Heat to boiling, stirring constantly. Boil and stir 1 minute; remove from heat. Stir in cheese until melted.

Place macaroni in ungreased 1¹/2-quart casserole. Stir cheese sauce into macaroni. Bake uncovered 30 minutes. *5 servings*

NUTRITION INFORMATION PER SERVING

ONE SERVING		PERCENT OF U.S. RDA	
Calories	365	Vitamin A	20%
Protein, g	15	Vitamin C	*
Carbohydrate, g	37	Calcium	28%
Fat, g	18	Iron	10%
Unsaturated	9		
Saturated	9		
Dietary fiber, g	1		
Cholesterol, mg	40		
Sodium, mg	930		

Vegetable Manicotti

Place cooked and drained manicotti shells in cold water to prevent stickiness when you fill them. Before filling, remove manicotti from water and let excess water drip off.

8 uncooked manicotti shells

1 teaspoon olive or vegetable oil

½ cup shredded carrot (about 1 medium)

½ cup shredded zucchini

½ cup sliced mushrooms (about 1½ ounces)

¼ cup sliced green onions (2 to 3 medium)

1 clove garlic, finely chopped

1 container (15 ounces) low-fat or regular ricotta cheese

¼ cup grated Parmesan cheese

2 tablespoons chopped fresh or 2 teaspoons dried basil leaves

2 egg whites

1 can (8 ounces) tomato sauce

½ cup shredded part-skim mozzarella cheese (2 ounces)

Heat oven to 350°. Grease rectangular baking dish, 11×7×1½ inches. Cook manicotti shells as directed on package; drain. Heat oil in 10-inch skillet over medium-high heat. Cook carrot, zucchini, mushrooms, onions and garlic in oil. Stir in ricotta cheese, Parmesan cheese, basil and egg whites.

Pour ⅓ cup of the tomato sauce in baking dish. Fill manicotti shells with vegetable mixture; place on tomato sauce in baking dish. Pour remaining tomato sauce over manicotti. Sprinkle with mozzarella cheese. Cover and bake 40 to 45 minutes or until hot and bubbly. *4 servings*

NUTRITION INFORMATION PER SERVING

ONE SERVING		PERCENT OF U.S. RDA	
Calories	334	Vitamin A	42%
Protein, g	24	Vitamin C	10%
Carbohydrate, g	30	Calcium	50%
Fat, g	14	Iron	14%
Unsaturated	6		
Saturated	8		
Dietary fiber, g	2		
Cholesterol, mg	45		
Sodium, mg	760		

Pasta Yields

One ounce of dried pasta will yield approximately ½ cup of cooked pasta. This will vary slightly depending on the shape, type and size of pasta.

Uncooked	Cooked	Servings
Macaroni 6 or 7 ounces (2 cups)	4 cups	4 to 6
Spaghetti 7 to 8 ounces	4 cups	4 to 6
Noodles 8 ounces (4 to 5 cups)	4 to 5 cups	4 to 6

Pasta Torte

2 tablespoons dry bread crumbs

1 package (12 ounces) mini lasagne (mafalda) pasta or wide egg noodles

1 cup shredded carrots (about 1½ medium)

2 cups broccoli flowerets

½ cup grated Parmesan cheese

¾ cup Egg Substitute (page 88) or cholesterol-free egg product or 3 eggs

½ cup milk

¼ teaspoon salt

¼ teaspoon pepper

1½ cups spaghetti sauce

Heat oven to 350°. Grease springform pan, 8×2 inches; sprinkle bread crumbs over bottom of pan. Cook pasta as directed on package; drain. Spread 2 cups cooked pasta in pan; top with 1 cup carrots. Arrange broccoli around outside edge of pasta. Sprinkle center with ½ cup carrots. Mix Egg Substitute, milk, salt and pepper; pour milk mixture over broccoli.

Bake covered 50 minutes. Sprinkle with cheese. Bake uncovered about 10 minutes longer or until set. Cool 10 minutes; remove side of pan. Cut torte into wedges. Serve with spaghetti sauce. *6 servings*

NUTRITION INFORMATION PER SERVING

ONE SERVING		PERCENT OF U.S. RDA	
Calories	325	Vitamin A	44%
Protein, g	16	Vitamin C	18%
Carbohydrate, g	57	Calcium	20%
Fat, g	6	Iron	20%
Unsaturated	4		
Saturated	2		
Dietary fiber, g	5		
Cholesterol, mg	5		
Sodium, mg	940		

Pasta e Fagioli Stew

5 cups hot cooked bow-tie (farfalle) pasta

4 cups cooked dried great northern beans or 2 cans (15 to 16 ounces each) great northern beans, rinsed and drained

1 tablespoon chopped fresh or 1 teaspoon dried sage leaves

¼ teaspoon pepper

1 can (15 ounces) tomato sauce

¼ cup soft whole wheat or white bread crumbs

1 tablespoon grated fresh Parmesan cheese

Heat oven to 375°. Grease 3-quart casserole. Mix all ingredients except bread crumbs and cheese; spoon into casserole. Sprinkle with bread crumbs and cheese. Bake uncovered about 30 minutes or until golden brown. *6 servings*

NUTRITION INFORMATION PER SERVING

ONE SERVING		PERCENT OF U.S. RDA	
Calories	345	Vitamin A	6%
Protein, g	19	Vitamin C	8%
Carbohydrate, g	72	Calcium	14%
Fat, g	2	Iron	38%
Unsaturated	1		
Saturated	1		
Dietary fiber, g	9		
Cholesterol, mg	0		
Sodium, mg	660		

Pasta Torte

Winter Baked Pasta

6 cups hot cooked tricolored wheel-shaped pasta

3 cups cooked broc-o-flowerets or broccoli flowerets (about 1 pound)

3 cups peeled chopped cooked acorn, buttercup or butternut squash

1/2 cup chopped green onions

1/2 cup chopped celery

2 cups milk

1 cup low-fat or regular ricotta cheese

1 teaspoon salt

1 tablespoon cornstarch

1/2 teaspoon pepper

1/4 teaspoon ground nutmeg

1 clove garlic, finely chopped

1/2 cup soft bread crumbs

2 tablespoons grated fresh Parmesan cheese

2 tablespoons shredded Gouda cheese

Heat oven to 375°. Grease 3-quart casserole. Mix pasta, broc-o-flowerets and squash. Mix milk, ricotta, cornstarch, salt, pepper and nutmeg. Pour over pasta, mix well. Spoon into casserole. Sprinkle with remaining ingredients. Bake uncovered about 35 minutes or until golden brown. *6 servings*

NUTRITION INFORMATION PER SERVING

ONE SERVING		PERCENT OF U.S. RDA	
Calories	390	Vitamin A	64%
Protein, g	20	Vitamin C	40%
Carbohydrate, g	67	Calcium	34%
Fat, g	8	Iron	20%
Unsaturated	4		
Saturated	4		
Dietary fiber, g	7		
Cholesterol, mg	25		
Sodium, mg	800		

Winter Baked Pasta

Mushroom and Spinach Lasagne

1 package (8 ounces) lasagne noodles

1 1/4 cups low-fat or regular ricotta cheese

1/2 cup Egg Substitute (page 88) or cholesterol-free egg product or 2 eggs

1 cup chopped mushrooms (about 4 ounces)

1/2 cup chopped onion (about 1 medium)

1 package (10 ounces) frozen chopped spinach, thawed and drained

1/2 teaspoon salt

1/4 teaspoon ground nutmeg

1 can (15 ounces) tomato sauce

3 tablespoons grated Parmesan cheese

Heat oven to 350°. Grease rectangular baking dish, 11×7×1 1/2 inches. Cook noodles as directed on package; drain. Mix 1/2 cup of the ricotta cheese, 1/4 cup of the Egg Substitute, the mushrooms and onion. Mix remaining 3/4 cup ricotta cheese, 1/4 cup Egg Substitute, the spinach, salt and nutmeg.

Spread 1/2 cup of the tomato sauce in baking dish. Top with 4 noodles, overlapping to fit. Layer with mushroom mixture, 3 noodles, spinach mixture, 3 noodles and remaining tomato sauce. Cover loosely with aluminum foil and bake 50 minutes. Sprinkle with Parmesan cheese. Bake uncovered about 10 minutes or until cheese browns. Let stand 10 minutes before cutting. *6 servings*

NUTRITION INFORMATION PER SERVING

ONE SERVING		PERCENT OF U.S. RDA	
Calories	270	Vitamin A	38%
Protein, g	16	Vitamin C	12%
Carbohydrate, g	41	Calcium	24%
Fat, g	6	Iron	24%
Unsaturated	3		
Saturated	3		
Dietary fiber, g	3		
Cholesterol, mg	20		
Sodium, mg	930		

Spinach-Fennel Kugel

Kugel, often referred to as noodle pudding, is a dish made of noodles or potatoes, eggs and milk.

6 cups hot cooked whole wheat or regular elbow macaroni

1 cup low-fat or regular ricotta cheese

1/2 cup chopped fresh fennel (about 1 medium bulb)

1/2 cup nonfat cream cheese product or regular cream cheese, softened

1/4 cup chopped red onion

1 cup milk

3/4 cup Egg Substitute (page 88) or cholesterol-free egg product or 3 eggs

2 teaspoons chopped fresh or 1/2 teaspoon dried dill weed

1 teaspoon salt

1/4 teaspoon pepper

1 package (10 ounces) frozen chopped spinach, thawed and drained

1/2 cup soft whole wheat or white bread crumbs

Heat oven to 375°. Grease pie plate, 10×1 1/2 inches. Mix all ingredients except bread crumbs; spoon into pie plate. Sprinkle with bread crumbs. Bake uncovered about 35 minutes or until golden brown. Let stand 10 minutes before cutting. *6 servings*

NUTRITION INFORMATION PER SERVING

ONE SERVING		PERCENT OF U.S. RDA	
Calories	390	Vitamin A	98%
Protein, g	24	Vitamin C	8%
Carbohydrate, g	56	Calcium	40%
Fat, g	9	Iron	22%
Unsaturated	6		
Saturated	3		
Dietary fiber, g	3		
Cholesterol, mg	25		
Sodium, mg	840		

Three-Cheese Noodle Bake

2 cups uncooked cholesterol-free or regular noodles

1 cup low-fat or regular cottage cheese

3/4 cup shredded reduced-fat or regular Cheddar cheese (3 ounces)

1/2 cup low-fat or regular sour cream

1/3 cup chopped green onions (about 3 medium)

3 tablespoons grated Parmesan cheese

1/2 teaspoon Worcestershire sauce

1/8 teaspoon pepper

2 egg whites

1 egg

Heat oven to 350°. Grease square baking dish, 8×8×2 inches. Cook noodles as directed on package; drain. Mix noodles and remaining ingredients. Spread in baking dish. Bake uncovered 30 to 35 minutes or until center is set and edges are golden brown. Let stand 5 minutes before serving. *4 servings*

NUTRITION INFORMATION PER SERVING

ONE SERVING		PERCENT OF U.S. RDA	
Calories	300	Vitamin A	12%
Protein, g	24	Vitamin C	*
Carbohydrate, g	30	Calcium	30%
Fat, g	10	Iron	8%
Unsaturated	4		
Saturated	6		
Dietary fiber, g	1		
Cholesterol, mg	80		
Sodium, mg	600		

Fall Vegetable Bake

2 cups low-fat or regular cottage cheese

1 cup soft whole wheat or white bread crumbs (about 1½ slices bread)

1 tablespoon chopped fresh or 1 teaspoon dried tarragon leaves

1 teaspoon salt

½ teaspoon pepper

3 egg whites

1 egg

2 cups ⅛-inch slices Jerusalem artichokes (about ½ pound)

2 cups finely chopped cauliflower (about 10 ounces)

2 cups shredded kohlrabi bulbs (about 2 pounds) or celeriac (about ½ large)

1 cup shredded parsnip (about 1 medium)

1 can (19 ounces) fava beans, rinsed and drained, or 1 can (15 to 16 ounces) butter beans, rinsed and drained

¼ cup chopped slivered almonds

Heat oven to 375°. Grease 3-quart casserole. Mix cottage cheese, bread crumbs, tarragon, salt, pepper, egg whites and egg in large bowl. Stir in remaining ingredients except almonds; spoon into casserole. Sprinkle with almonds. Bake uncovered 25 to 30 minutes or until golden brown. Let stand 5 minutes before serving. *6 servings*

NUTRITION INFORMATION PER SERVING

ONE SERVING		PERCENT OF U.S. RDA	
Calories	320	Vitamin A	4%
Protein, g	24	Vitamin C	20%
Carbohydrate, g	51	Calcium	14%
Fat, g	6	Iron	16%
Unsaturated	4		
Saturated	2		
Dietary fiber, g	9		
Cholesterol, mg	45		
Sodium, mg	910		

Phyllo and Spinach Pie

1 cup low-fat or regular ricotta cheese

1 cup chopped green onions (about 10 medium)

⅓ cup crumbled feta cheese

½ cup Egg Substitute (page 88) or cholesterol-free egg product or 2 eggs

1 tablespoon chopped fresh or 1 teaspoon dried dill weed

2 tablespoons lemon juice

½ teaspoon pepper

1 package (10 ounces) frozen chopped spinach, thawed and drained

1 tablespoon vegetable or olive oil

1 tablespoon margarine or butter

2 frozen phyllo sheets, thawed

Heat oven to 400°. Grease rectangular baking dish, 11×7×1½ inches. Mix all ingredients except oil, margarine and phyllo. Heat oil and margarine in 1-quart saucepan over low heat until melted. Arrange phyllo in baking dish, overlapping slightly and with edges extending over sides of dish. Brush phyllo with 1 tablespoon margarine mixture.

Spoon spinach mixture over phyllo and smooth top. Fold phyllo over top, completely enclosing spinach mixture. Brush with remaining margarine mixture. Bake 20 to 25 minutes or until golden brown. *6 servings*

NUTRITION INFORMATION PER SERVING

ONE SERVING		PERCENT OF U.S. RDA	
Calories	145	Vitamin A	10%
Protein, g	8	Vitamin C	2%
Carbohydrate, g	9	Calcium	16%
Fat, g	9	Iron	6%
Unsaturated	5		
Saturated	4		
Dietary fiber, g	1		
Cholesterol, mg	20		
Sodium, mg	210		

Vegetable Shepherd's Pie

Serve with hot, toasted garlic bread, and you'll increase the protein in this meal.

4 cups shredded red cabbage (about 1 pound)

3 cups chopped leeks with tops (about 6 medium)

1 cup chopped mushrooms (about 4 ounces)

1 cup chopped parsnip (about 1 large)

1 cup apple juice or Roasted Vegetable Broth (page 15)

2 teaspoons chopped fresh or ¹/₂ teaspoon dried thyme leaves

1 teaspoon salt

1 can (15 to 16 ounces) garbanzo beans, rinsed and drained

2 tablespoons tahini (sesame seed paste)*

2 tablespoons lemon juice

3 egg whites

¹/₃ cup low-fat or regular sour cream

¹/₂ teaspoon pepper

2 cups coarsely chopped cooked potatoes (about 2 medium)

1 tablespoon grated Parmesan cheese

Heat oven to 400°. Grease 3-quart casserole. Heat cabbage, leeks, mushrooms, parsnip, apple juice, thyme and salt to boiling in 3-quart saucepan over medium-high heat, stirring occasionally; reduce heat to medium-low. Cook 10 minutes or until leeks are softened and liquid is absorbed.

Meanwhile, place beans, tahini and lemon juice in blender or food processor. Cover and blend slightly or process until mixture is a chunky puree. Stir bean puree into cabbage mixture; spoon into casserole. Beat egg whites, sour cream and pepper, using wire whisk, until smooth; spoon over cabbage mixture. Spread potatoes over sour cream mixture. Sprinkle with cheese. Bake uncovered about 45 minutes or until set and golden brown. *6 servings*

* Tahini may be purchased at specialty and health food stores, as well as at most grocery stores.

NUTRITION INFORMATION PER SERVING

ONE SERVING		PERCENT OF U.S. RDA	
Calories	250	Vitamin A	4%
Protein, g	12	Vitamin C	32%
Carbohydrate, g	45	Calcium	16%
Fat, g	6	Iron	22%
Unsaturated	4		
Saturated	2		
Dietary fiber, g	8		
Cholesterol, mg	5		
Sodium, mg	610		

Winter Root Vegetable Casserole

Chase away the winter chills by serving this savory casserole with a glass of milk and whole-grain bread.

3¹/₂ cups hot cooked brown or regular long grain rice

2 cups cooked Brussels sprouts (about ¹/₂ pound)

2 cups shredded kohlrabi bulbs (about 2 pounds) or celeriac (about ¹/₂ large)

1 cup chopped celery (about 2 medium stalks)

1 cup shredded carrots (about 1¹/₂ medium)

2 tablespoons soy sauce

1 tablespoon Dijon mustard

¹/₄ teaspoon pepper

3 egg whites

1 egg

¹/₄ cup shredded Monterey Jack cheese (1 ounce)

Heat oven to 350°. Grease 3-quart casserole. Mix all ingredients except cheese; spoon into casserole. Sprinkle with cheese. Bake uncovered 30 to 35 minutes or until golden brown. *6 servings*

NUTRITION INFORMATION PER SERVING

ONE SERVING		PERCENT OF U.S. RDA	
Calories	195	Vitamin A	34%
Protein, g	10	Vitamin C	46%
Carbohydrate, g	37	Calcium	8%
Fat, g	4	Iron	8%
Unsaturated	2		
Saturated	2		
Dietary fiber, g	7		
Cholesterol, mg	40		
Sodium, mg	810		

Savory Bread Pudding

2 cups milk

1 cup low-fat or regular ricotta cheese

2 tablespoons pesto

¹/₄ teaspoon pepper

2 egg yolks

7 slices whole wheat or white sandwich bread, torn into 2-inch pieces (about 4 cups)

1¹/₂ cups chopped broccoli flowerets

1 cup frozen whole kernel corn

¹/₂ cup chopped green onions (about 5 medium)

¹/₂ cup shredded reduced-fat or regular Monterey Jack cheese (2 ounces)

5 egg whites

Heat oven to 400°. Grease 3-quart casserole. Mix milk, ricotta cheese, pesto, pepper and egg yolks in large bowl. Stir in bread. Let stand 10 minutes. Stir in remaining ingredients except egg whites. Beat egg whites until stiff but not dry; fold into bread mixture. Gently spoon into casserole and smooth top. Bake uncovered 35 to 40 minutes or until set and golden brown. *6 servings.*

NUTRITION INFORMATION PER SERVING

ONE SERVING		PERCENT OF U.S. RDA	
Calories	285	Vitamin A	16%
Protein, g	19	Vitamin C	18%
Carbohydrate, g	30	Calcium	34%
Fat, g	11	Iron	10%
Unsaturated	6		
Saturated	5		
Dietary fiber, g	3		
Cholesterol, mg	95		
Sodium, mg	410		

Spicy Five-Pepper Spoon Bread

1 cup yellow cornmeal

2 cups milk

2 cups water

¹/₂ cup shredded Gruyère or Swiss cheese
(2 ounces)

1 cup frozen whole kernel corn

1 cup chopped yellow bell pepper (about 1
medium)

¹/₂ cup chopped red bell pepper (about 1
small)

¹/₂ cup chopped green bell pepper (about 1
small)

¹/₂ cup chopped onion (about 1 medium)

¹/₂ teaspoon salt

¹/₄ teaspoon white pepper

1 can (4 ounces) chopped green chiles,
drained

1 egg

3 egg whites

1 cup salsa

Heat oven to 400°. Grease 3-quart casserole. Mix cornmeal, milk and water in 2-quart saucepan. Cook, stirring constantly, until mixture thickens and boils; reduce heat. Stir in ¹/₄ cup of the cheese and the remaining ingredients except 3 egg whites and the salsa. Beat egg whites on high speed until soft peaks form; fold into cornmeal mixture. Spoon into casserole (casserole will be full). Sprinkle with remaining cheese. Bake uncovered 35 to 40 minutes or until set and golden brown. Serve with salsa. *4 servings*

NUTRITION INFORMATION PER SERVING

ONE SERVING		PERCENT OF U.S. RDA	
Calories	335	Vitamin A	36%
Protein, g	18	Vitamin C	74%
Carbohydrate, g	53	Calcium	30%
Fat, g	8	Iron	16%
Unsaturated	3		
Saturated	5		
Dietary fiber, g	5		
Cholesterol, mg	75		
Sodium, mg	1380		

Spicy Five-Pepper Spoon Bread

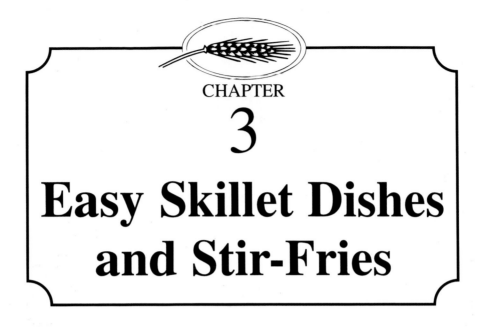

CHAPTER

3

Easy Skillet Dishes and Stir-Fries

S tir-fries and other skillet dishes are always popular, as they make the most of your time in the kitchen, providing speedy suppers that don't skimp on taste. You'll appreciate the variety of dishes here—exotic Moroccan Garbanzo Beans with Raisins, down-home Texas Red Beans and Rice or family-pleasing Double Spinach Fettuccine. We think you'll find your skillet is more popular than ever with these time-saving recipes.

Texas Red Beans and Rice (*page 61*)

Crunchy Bean Skillet

1 cup sliced celery (about 2 medium stalks)

½ cup sliced green onions (about 5 medium)

1 tablespoon chopped fresh or 1 teaspoon parsley flakes

1 tablespoon chopped fresh or 1 teaspoon dried basil leaves

2 teaspoons chopped fresh or ½ teaspoon dried oregano leaves

3 cans (15 to 16 ounces each) cannellini beans, rinsed and drained

1 jar (14 ounces) spaghetti sauce

1 cup shredded part-skim or regular mozzarella cheese (4 ounces)

½ cup coarsely chopped walnuts

Mix all ingredients except cheese and walnuts in 10-inch skillet. Heat to boiling; reduce heat. Sprinkle with cheese. Cover and simmer 3 to 5 minutes or just until cheese is melted. Sprinkle with walnuts. *6 servings*

NUTRITION INFORMATION PER SERVING

ONE SERVING		PERCENT OF U.S. RDA	
Calories	330	Vitamin A	8%
Protein, g	21	Vitamin C	16%
Carbohydrate, g	47	Calcium	24%
Fat, g	13	Iron	32%
Unsaturated	10		
Saturated	3		
Dietary fiber, g	15		
Cholesterol, mg	10		
Sodium, mg	1000		

Moroccan Garbanzo Beans with Raisins

Try this Middle Eastern skillet meal with Indian naan, or flat bread.

½ cup chopped onion (about 1 medium)

1 large onion, sliced

1 clove garlic, finely chopped

2 tablespoons vegetable oil

1 cup peeled diced acorn, buttercup or butternut squash

½ cup raisins

1 cup chicken broth or Roasted Vegetable Broth (page 15)

1 teaspoon ground turmeric

1 teaspoon ground cinnamon

½ teaspoon ground ginger

1 can (15 to 16 ounces) garbanzo beans, rinsed and drained

2 cups hot cooked brown or regular long grain rice

Cook chopped onion, sliced onion and garlic in oil in 3-quart saucepan about 7 minutes, stirring occasionally, until onion is crisp-tender. Stir in remaining ingredients except beans and rice. Heat to boiling; reduce heat. Cover and simmer about 8 minutes or until squash is tender. Stir in beans. Serve over rice. *4 servings*

NUTRITION INFORMATION PER SERVING

ONE SERVING		PERCENT OF U.S. RDA	
Calories	405	Vitamin A	18%
Protein, g	12	Vitamin C	16%
Carbohydrate, g	75	Calcium	8%
Fat, g	10	Iron	26%
Unsaturated	8		
Saturated	2		
Dietary fiber, g	8		
Cholesterol, mg	0		
Sodium, mg	770		

Black Bean Enchiladas

1 teaspoon vegetable oil

1/2 cup chopped onion (about 1 medium)

1 clove garlic, crushed

1 cup nonfat or regular sour cream

1 tablespoon lime juice

1/2 teaspoon ground cumin

2 cans (15 ounces each) black beans, rinsed, drained and mashed

8 whole wheat or regular flour tortillas (7 inches in diameter)

1 can (15 ounces) tomato sauce

1/2 cup shredded Monterey Jack cheese with jalapeño chiles (2 ounces)

Heat oil in 10-inch skillet over medium-high heat. Cook onion and garlic in oil about 2 minutes, stirring occasionally, until onion is crisp-tender. Stir in sour cream, lime juice, cumin and beans. Spoon about 1/3 cup bean mixture onto each tortilla. Roll tortilla around filling; place seam side down in skillet. Pour tomato sauce over enchiladas. Sprinkle with cheese. Cook over low heat 10 to 15 minutes or until hot and bubbly. *4 servings*

NUTRITION INFORMATION PER SERVING

ONE SERVING		PERCENT OF U.S. RDA	
Calories	390	Vitamin A	30%
Protein, g	26	Vitamin C	50%
Carbohydrate, g	74	Calcium	38%
Fat, g	3	Iron	38%
Unsaturated	2		
Saturated	1		
Dietary fiber, g	9		
Cholesterol, mg	5		
Sodium, mg	830		

Texas Red Beans and Rice

2 teaspoons vegetable oil

1/2 cup chopped onion (about 1 medium)

3/4 cup chopped green bell pepper (about 1 medium)

2 cloves garlic, crushed

2 teaspoons chopped fresh or 1/2 teaspoon dried thyme leaves

1/2 teaspoon salt

1/2 teaspoon red pepper sauce

2 cans (15 to 16 ounces each) kidney beans, rinsed and drained

1 package (10 ounces) frozen cut okra, thawed

1 cup frozen whole kernel corn, thawed

4 cups hot cooked rice

Heat oil in 10-inch skillet over medium-high heat. Cook onion, bell pepper and garlic in oil about 2 minutes, stirring occasionally. Stir in remaining ingredients except rice. Cook, stirring occasionally, until mixture is hot. Serve with rice. Top with tomato. *4 servings*

NUTRITION INFORMATION PER SERVING

ONE SERVING		PERCENT OF U.S. RDA	
Calories	455	Vitamin A	6%
Protein, g	20	Vitamin C	50%
Carbohydrate, g	101	Calcium	12%
Fat, g	4	Iron	40%
Unsaturated	3		
Saturated	1		
Dietary fiber, g	16		
Cholesterol, mg	0		
Sodium, mg	1410		

Caribbean Black Beans

4¹/₂ cups water

1¹/₂ cups dried black beans*

2 teaspoons vegetable oil

1 cup finely chopped red bell pepper (about 1 medium)

¹/₂ cup finely chopped red onion (about ¹/₂ medium)

¹/₂ cup orange juice

¹/₄ cup lime juice

2 tablespoons chopped fresh cilantro

¹/₂ teaspoon ground red pepper (cayenne)

1 medium papaya, peeled, seeded and diced

2 cloves garlic, crushed

5 cups hot cooked rice

Heat water and beans to boiling in 2-quart saucepan. Boil uncovered 2 minutes; reduce heat. Cover and simmer about 45 minutes, stirring occasionally, until beans are tender; drain and set aside.

Heat oil in 10-inch skillet over medium heat. Cook remaining ingredients except rice and beans in oil about 5 minutes, stirring occasionally, until bell pepper is crisp-tender. Stir in beans. Cook about 5 minutes or until hot. Serve with rice. *5 servings*

* 2 cans (15 ounces each) black beans, rinsed and drained, can be substituted for the dried black beans; do not cook in water.

NUTRITION INFORMATION PER SERVING

ONE SERVING		PERCENT OF U.S. RDA	
Calories	480	Vitamin A	14%
Protein, g	19	Vitamin C	76%
Carbohydrate, g	107	Calcium	14%
Fat, g	3	Iron	34%
Unsaturated	2		
Saturated	1		
Dietary fiber, g	13		
Cholesterol, mg	0		
Sodium, mg	790		

Stuffed Cabbage

Parsley buttered noodles would go nicely with these cabbage rolls stuffed full of grain and black-eyed peas.

1 small head green cabbage (about 1 pound)

1³/₄ cups water

³/₄ cup uncooked quinoa

1 teaspoon margarine or butter

¹/₂ cup chopped onion (about 1 medium)

1 can (15 to 16 ounces) black-eyed peas, rinsed and drained

1 can (4 ounces) chopped green chiles, drained

1 can (15 ounces) tomato sauce with tomato bits

Remove core from cabbage. Cover cabbage with cold water; let stand about 10 minutes. Remove 12 cabbage leaves. Cover leaves with boiling water. Cover and let stand until leaves are limp, about 10 minutes; drain.

Heat 1³/₄ cups water and the quinoa to boiling in 2-quart saucepan; reduce heat. Cover and simmer

10 to 15 minutes or until centers of quinoa grains are translucent and liquid is absorbed; drain if necessary.

Heat margarine in 10-inch skillet over medium heat. Cook onion in margarine about 1 minute, stirring occasionally, until onion is crisp-tender. Stir in quinoa, peas and chiles. Spoon about ¼ cup quinoa mixture onto each cabbage leaf. Fold sides of leaf over filling and roll up; place seam sides down in skillet. Pour tomato sauce over cabbage packets. Cover and cook over low heat 10 to 12 minutes or until cabbage is hot. *6 servings*

NUTRITION INFORMATION PER SERVING

ONE SERVING		PERCENT OF U.S. RDA	
Calories	160	Vitamin A	18%
Protein, g	9	Vitamin C	24%
Carbohydrate, g	34	Calcium	8%
Fat, g	2	Iron	24%
Unsaturated	1		
Saturated	1		
Dietary fiber, g	8		
Cholesterol, mg	0		
Sodium, mg	430		

Vegetable Sauté with Black Beans and Couscous

1 teaspoon olive or vegetable oil

1 medium red onion, thinly sliced

1 large red bell pepper, cut crosswise in half and thinly sliced

1 small bulb fennel, cut into fourths and thinly sliced

2 tablespoons chopped fresh or 2 teaspoons dried oregano leaves

¼ teaspoon crushed red pepper

2 cans (15 ounces each) black beans, rinsed and drained

2 cups hot cooked couscous
Plain yogurt, if desired

Heat oil in 10-inch skillet over medium-high heat. Cook onion, bell pepper and fennel in oil 2 to 3 minutes, stirring occasionally, until crisp-tender. Stir in oregano, red pepper and beans; reduce heat. Simmer uncovered 5 minutes. Serve with couscous. Garnish with yogurt. *4 servings*

NUTRITION INFORMATION PER SERVING

ONE SERVING		PERCENT OF U.S. RDA	
Calories	355	Vitamin A	10%
Protein, g	19	Vitamin C	50%
Carbohydrate, g	78	Calcium	12%
Fat, g	2	Iron	26%
Unsaturated	2		
Saturated	0		
Dietary fiber, g	13		
Cholesterol, mg	0		
Sodium, mg	350		

Know Your Grains

There are many grains available to us today from whole kernels to finely ground flours. Grains add color, texture and flavor to foods while providing many benefits, such as fiber. When grains are combined with dairy products or beans, peas or lentils, they provide high-quality protein.

Rinse grains in water before cooking. Be sure to use an extra-fine mesh strainer for small grains such as quinoa. Grains lose moisture with age, so you may need more or less water than the recipe calls for. If all water is absorbed but the grain isn't quite tender, add a little more liquid and cook longer. If grain is tender but all the liquid hasn't been absorbed, just drain. Cooked grains can be covered and refrigerated for up to a week.

Barley was one of the first grains ever cultivated. Pearl barley, the most commonly available, has had the hull, most of the bran and some of the germ removed to shorten the cooking time. It contains niacin, thiamin and potassium. One cup of cooked barley provides the same amount of protein as a glass of milk.

Buckwheat kernels, also called roasted buckwheat kernels or groats, are hulled seeds of the buckwheat plant. Roasted groats are often called *kasha*. Technically a fruit, buckwheat is used as a grain. It contains phosphorus, iron, potassium, vitamin E and B vitamins. It has a pungent flavor that can be overpowering. Buckwheat flour is usually mixed with all-purpose flour for pastas, pancakes, muffins and quick breads.

Corn is sometimes forgotten as a grain because we usually eat it as a vegetable. Paired with legumes or small amounts of animal protein from dairy products or eggs, corn provides a complete protein.

Cornmeal is available in degerminated and whole-grain forms. As *degerminated* indicates, the germ and bran have been removed. It is available at grocery stores. Stone-ground whole grain cornmeal may be a little harder to come by. It contains the germ and the bran, which gives it more flavor, texture and fiber. Look for whole grain cornmeal at health food stores or a local mill. Degerminated cornmeal can be stored at room temperature. Store whole grain cornmeal in a moisture-proof, vapor-proof plastic bag in refrigerator or freezer. If whole grain cornmeal is stored at room temperature, use within six to eight months.

Couscous ("KOOS-koos") is a staple of North African and some Middle Eastern cuisines. Couscous is actually granular semolina (coarsely ground durum wheat) and is often used in place of rice. A distinct advantage to couscous is its quick cooking time—five minutes.

Oats that we eat as oatmeal are steamed and flattened groats (hulled oat kernels) and are called rolled oats. They are available either regular (old-fashioned), quick-cooking or instant. Regular and quick-cooking oats are often used interchangeably. If a recipe specifies just one, however, do not substitute the other—they have different absorption properties. Oats contribute fiber, thiamin, phosphorus and magnesium.

Quinoa ("keen-wa") was once the staple of the Inca Indians in Peru. It is a small grain with a soft crunch and can be used in any recipe calling for rice. Be sure to rinse it well before cooking to remove the bitter-tasting, naturally occurring saponin (nature's insect repellent) that forms on the outside of the kernel. Quinoa provides B vitamins, calcium, iron and phosphorus and, unlike other grains, is a complete protein.

Brown Rice is unpolished, meaning the outer hull has been removed, but the germ and bran layers have not been "polished" off. This gives it a nutlike flavor and chewier texture than white rice. It is also a good source of fiber and thiamin.

Wild Rice is actually not rice, but an aquatic grass native to North America. It is more expensive than true rices because of its limited supply. Stretch it by mixing with other rices or grains. Purchase less expensive packages of broken kernels, when you find them, to use in soups and quick breads. Wild rice contains fiber, B vitamins, iron, phosphorus, magnesium, calcium and zinc.

Rye Flour is labeled "light" or "dark." The light flour has been sifted and most of the bran has been removed. Dark flour is sometimes referred to as "pumpernickel flour." Although it is a very flavorful bread flour, it doesn't have much gluten, which is the protein that gives bread dough its structure during rising and it should be blended with wheat flour for baking. Store rye flour in a moisture-proof, vapor-proof plastic bag in refrigerator or freezer. If flour is stored at room temperature, use within six to eight months.

Wheat Berries are hulled whole grain wheat kernels that still have the bran and germ. Cooked wheat berries can be used like rice in salads and side dishes. Wheat provides B vitamins, vitamin E and complex carbohydrates. Combining wheat with legumes or dairy products provides a complete protein.

Wheat Bulgur is whole wheat that's been cooked, dried and then broken into coarse fragments. It's different from cracked wheat because it is precooked. Bulgur supplies phosphorus and potassium and also contains some iron, thiamin and riboflavin.

Whole Wheat Flour is ground from the whole wheat kernel, usually from hard spring wheat, and adds a nutty flavor to baked goods. Whole wheat flour contains the oil-rich germ of the wheat kernel. To protect its flavor, store flour in a moisture-proof, vapor-proof plastic bag in refrigerator or freezer. If flour is stored at room temperature, use within six to eight months.

Barley *Wheat Berries* *Brown Rice*

Bulgar *Buckwheat Kernels (Kasha)* *Wild Rice* *Quinoa*

Cornmeal *Couscous* *Rye Flour*

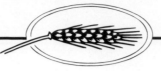

Rice and Grains
Cooking Chart

Rinse grains in water before cooking (except couscous), and be sure to use an extra-fine mesh strainer for small grains such as quinoa. Grains lose moisture with age, so you may find that you need more or less liquid than the recipe calls for. If all the liquid is absorbed but the grain isn't quite tender, add a little more liquid and cook longer. If it is tender but all the liquid hasn't been absorbed, just drain. Cooked grains can be covered and refrigerated for up to a week.

TYPE OF UNCOOKED GRAIN	AMOUNT OF COOKING LIQUID	METHOD OF COOKING (USING 2-QUART SAUCEPAN WITH LID)	APPROXIMATE COOKING TIME	APPROXIMATE YIELD
Brown Rice (1 cup)	2¾ cups	Heat rice and liquid to a boil. Reduce heat. Cover and simmer.	45 to 50 minutes	4 cups
Regular Rice (1 cup)	2 cups	Heat rice and liquid to a boil. Reduce heat. Cover and simmer.	15 minutes	3 cups
Wild Rice (1 cup)	2½ cups	Heat rice and liquid to a boil. Reduce heat. Cover and simmer.	40 to 50 minutes	3 cups
Parboiled Rice (converted) (1 cup)	2½ cups	Heat liquid to a boil. Stir in rice. Reduce heat. Cover and simmer.	20 minutes. Remove from heat. Let stand covered 5 minutes.	3 to 4 cups
Precooked White Rice (instant) (1 cup)	1 cup	Heat liquid to a boil. Stir in rice. Cover and remove from heat.	Let stand covered 5 minutes.	2 cups

TYPE OF UNCOOKED GRAIN	AMOUNT OF COOKING LIQUID	METHOD OF COOKING (USING 2-QUART SAUCEPAN WITH LID)	APPROXIMATE COOKING TIME	APPROXIMATE YIELD
Precooked Brown Rice (instant) (1 cup)	1¼ cups	Heat liquid to a boil. Stir in rice. Reduce heat. Cover and simmer.	10 minutes	2 cups
Barley (regular) (1 cup)	4 cups	Heat liquid to a boil. Stir in barley. Reduce heat. Cover and simmer.	45 to 50 minutes. Let stand covered 5 minutes.	4 cups
Barley (quick-cooking) (1 cup)	2 cups	Heat liquid to a boil. Stir in barley. Reduce heat. Cover and simmer.	10 to 12 minutes. Let stand covered 5 minutes.	3 cups
Bulgur (1 cup)	3 cups	Pour boiling liquid over bulgur and soak. Do not cook.	Soak 30 to 60 minutes.	3 cups
Couscous (1 cup)	1½ cups	Heat liquid to a boil. Stir in couscous. Cover and remove from heat.	Let stand covered 5 minutes.	3 to 3½ cups
Kasha (roasted buckwheat kernels) (1 cup)	2 cups	Pour boiling liquid over kasha and soak. Do not cook.	Soak 10 to 15 minutes.	4 cups
Quinoa (1 cup)	2 cups	Heat quinoa and liquid to a boil. Reduce heat. Cover and simmer.	15 minutes	3 to 4 cups
Wheat Berries (1 cup)	2½ cups	Heat wheat berries and liquid to a boil. Reduce heat. Cover and simmer.	50 to 60 minutes	2¾ to 3 cups

Spring Vegetable Paella

1 pound asparagus, cut into 2-inch pieces

3 cups broccoli flowerets

2 teaspoons olive or vegetable oil

1 medium red bell pepper cut into ¼-inch strips

1¼ cups sliced zucchini (about 1 medium)

½ cup chopped onion (about 1 medium)

4 cups cooked brown or regular long grain rice

2 cups coarsely chopped seeded tomatoes (about 2 large)

¾ teaspoon salt

½ teaspoon saffron threads or ¼ teaspoon ground turmeric

2 cans (15 to 16 ounces each) garbanzo beans, rinsed and drained

1 package (10 ounces) frozen green peas, thawed

Cook asparagus and broccoli in enough boiling water to cover in 2-quart saucepan about 4 minutes or until crisp-tender; drain.

Heat oil in Dutch oven over medium-high heat. Cook asparagus, broccoli, bell pepper, zucchini and onion in oil about 5 minutes, stirring occasionally, until onion is crisp-tender. Stir in remaining ingredients. Cook about 5 minutes, stirring frequently, until hot. *6 servings*

NUTRITION INFORMATION PER SERVING

ONE SERVING		PERCENT OF U.S. RDA	
Calories	280	Vitamin A	30%
Protein, g	13	Vitamin C	75%
Carbohydrate, g	58	Calcium	10%
Fat, g	4	Iron	24%
Unsaturated	3		
Saturated	1		
Dietary fiber, g	10		
Cholesterol, mg	0		
Sodium, mg	640		

Spring Vegetable Paella

Spicy Vegetables with Rice

1 tablespoon vegetable oil

¼ cup chopped green onions

1 tablespoon chopped gingerroot or ½ teaspoon ground ginger

4 cloves garlic, crushed

¼ cup chicken broth or Roasted Vegetable Broth (page 15)

1 teaspoon curry powder

½ teaspoon salt

⅛ teaspoon ground red pepper (cayenne)

1¼ cups chopped zucchini (about 2 small)

1 small eggplant (about 1 pound), cut into 1-inch pieces

1 small red bell pepper, thinly sliced

1 small green bell pepper, thinly sliced

2 cans (15 to 16 ounces each) cannellini beans, rinsed and drained

3 cups hot cooked basmati or regular long grain rice

Heat oil in 10-inch skillet over medium-high heat. Cook onions, gingerroot and garlic in oil 2 minutes, stirring occasionally. Stir in remaining ingredients except beans and rice. Cook about 5 minutes, stirring frequently, until vegetables are crisp-tender. Stir in beans. Cook until thoroughly heated. Serve with rice. *6 servings*

NUTRITION INFORMATION PER SERVING

ONE SERVING		PERCENT OF U.S. RDA	
Calories	270	Vitamin A	40%
Protein, g	12	Vitamin C	40%
Carbohydrate, g	59	Calcium	6%
Fat, g	3	Iron	26%
Unsaturated	2		
Saturated	1		
Dietary fiber, g	10		
Cholesterol, mg	0		
Sodium, mg	840		

Sautéed Bean Cakes with Tomato Salsa

*4¹/₄ cups soft whole wheat or white bread
  crumbs (about 6 slices bread)*

¹/₂ cup chopped fresh parsley

¹/₂ cup plain nonfat or regular yogurt

1 tablespoon Dijon mustard

1 tablespoon lemon juice

2 green onions, finely chopped

2 egg whites

*2 cans (15 to 16 ounces each) great
  northern beans, rinsed, drained and
  mashed*

1 tablespoon margarine or butter

Tomato Salsa (right)

Mix 3¹/₂ cups of the bread crumbs, the parsley, yogurt, mustard, lemon juice, onions, egg whites and beans. Shape into 12 3¹/₂-inch patties. Coat patties with remaining bread crumbs.

Heat margarine in 12-inch skillet over medium heat. Cook patties in margarine 5 to 6 minutes, turning after 3 minutes, until golden brown. Serve with Tomato Salsa. Garnish with guacamole if desired. *6 servings*

TOMATO SALSA

2 cups chopped tomatoes (about 2 large)

2 tablespoons chopped fresh cilantro

2 tablespoons red wine vinegar

¹/₄ teaspoon salt

Mix all ingredients.

NUTRITION INFORMATION PER SERVING

ONE SERVING		PERCENT OF U.S. RDA	
Calories	430	Vitamin A	8%
Protein, g	21	Vitamin C	18%
Carbohydrate, g	82	Calcium	22%
Fat, g	6	Iron	40%
Unsaturated	5		
Saturated	1		
Dietary fiber, g	9		
Cholesterol, mg	5		
Sodium, mg	940		

*Sautéed Bean Cakes with Tomato Salsa,
Vegetable Sauté with Black Beans and Couscous
(page 63)*

Curried Lentils and Barley

2 teaspoons vegetable oil

¹/₂ cup chopped onion (about 1 medium)

¹/₃ cup coarsely chopped red or green bell pepper

3¹/₂ cups water

¹/₂ cup uncooked pearled barley

1¹/₂ teaspoons curry powder

³/₄ teaspoon salt

1 cup thinly sliced carrots (about 2 medium)

³/₄ cup dried lentils

¹/₂ cup plain nonfat or regular yogurt

¹/₄ cup chutney

Heat oil in 3-quart saucepan over medium-high heat. Cook onion and bell pepper in oil, stirring occasionally, until onion is crisp-tender. Stir in water, barley, curry powder and salt. Heat to boiling; reduce heat. Cover and simmer 15 minutes. Stir in carrots and lentils. Heat to boiling; reduce heat. Cover and simmer 40 to 45 minutes, stirring occasionally, until lentils are tender and liquid is absorbed. Mix yogurt and chutney. Serve with lentil mixture. *4 servings*

NUTRITION INFORMATION PER SERVING

ONE SERVING		PERCENT OF U.S. RDA	
Calories	265	Vitamin A	62%
Protein, g	14	Vitamin C	20%
Carbohydrate, g	55	Calcium	10%
Fat, g	3	Iron	26%
Unsaturated	2		
Saturated	1		
Dietary fiber, g	10		
Cholesterol, mg	0		
Sodium, mg	460		

Squash-and-Lentil Risotto

1 tablespoon margarine or butter

¹/₂ cup chopped onion (about 1 medium)

1 cup uncooked Arborio or other short grain rice

2 cups peeled 1-inch pieces butternut squash (about 1 medium)

1 cup dried lentils

4 cups chicken broth or Vegetable Broth (page 14)

¹/₂ teaspoon ground nutmeg

¹/₄ teaspoon salt

¹/₄ cup grated Parmesan cheese

Heat margarine in 10-inch skillet over medium heat. Cook onion and rice in margarine 2 minutes, stirring occasionally. Stir in remaining ingredients except cheese. Heat to boiling; stir once thoroughly and reduce heat. Cover and simmer 20 to 25 minutes or until rice is tender and liquid is absorbed. Stir in cheese. Cover and let stand 5 minutes. *4 servings*

NUTRITION INFORMATION PER SERVING

ONE SERVING		PERCENT OF U.S. RDA	
Calories	435	Vitamin A	40%
Protein, g	24	Vitamin C	22%
Carbohydrate, g	80	Calcium	14%
Fat, g	7	Iron	40%
Unsaturated	5		
Saturated	2		
Dietary fiber, g	11		
Cholesterol, mg	5		
Sodium, mg	1580		

Lentil Ratatouille

2 tablespoons vegetable oil

4 cups diced eggplant (about 2 medium)

2 cups chopped zucchini (about 2 medium)

1 cup chopped red bell pepper (about 1 medium)

1/2 cup chopped onion (about 1 medium)

2 cloves garlic, crushed

2 tablespoons chopped fresh or 2 teaspoons dried basil leaves

1/4 teaspoon salt

1/4 teaspoon pepper

1 can (28 ounces) Italian plum tomatoes, undrained

4 cups cooked lentils

Heat oil in 10-inch skillet over medium-high heat. Cook eggplant, zucchini, bell pepper, onion and garlic in oil about 4 minutes, stirring occasionally, until vegetables are crisp-tender. Stir in remaining ingredients except lentils, breaking up tomatoes; reduce heat. Simmer uncovered 10 to 15 minutes to blend flavors. Stir in lentils. Cook until thoroughly heated. *4 servings*

NUTRITION INFORMATION PER SERVING

ONE SERVING		PERCENT OF U.S. RDA	
Calories	395	Vitamin A	22%
Protein, g	23	Vitamin C	75%
Carbohydrate, g	74	Calcium	14%
Fat, g	9	Iron	52%
Unsaturated	8		
Saturated	1		
Dietary fiber, g	19		
Cholesterol, mg	0		
Sodium, mg	470		

Indian Split Peas with Vegetables

2 teaspoons vegetable oil

1/2 teaspoon cumin seed or 1/4 teaspoon ground cumin

1/4 teaspoon ground turmeric

2 jalapeño chiles, seeded and chopped

3 cups cauliflowerets (about 1 pound)

1/4 cup chicken broth or Vegetable Broth (page 14)

2 cups cooked yellow split peas

2 cups frozen green peas, thawed

1 can (15 ounces) black beans, rinsed and drained

Heat oil in 10-inch skillet over medium-high heat. Cook cumin, turmeric and chiles in oil 2 minutes, stirring occasionally. Stir in cauliflowerets and broth. Cover and cook 3 to 4 minutes or until cauliflowerets are tender. Stir in remaining ingredients. Cook about 5 minutes, stirring occasionally, until hot. *4 servings*

NUTRITION INFORMATION PER SERVING

ONE SERVING		PERCENT OF U.S. RDA	
Calories	275	Vitamin A	24%
Protein, g	20	Vitamin C	100%
Carbohydrate, g	54	Calcium	10%
Fat, g	4	Iron	26%
Unsaturated	3		
Saturated	1		
Dietary fiber, g	14		
Cholesterol, mg	0		
Sodium, mg	300		

Polenta with Italian Vegetables

Try a side dish of vermicelli tossed with marinara sauce and a few slices of ripe olive to complete this satisfying dinner.

1 cup yellow cornmeal

³/₄ cup cold water

2¹/₂ cups boiling water

¹/₂ teaspoon salt

2 cups sliced yellow squash

1 cup sliced zucchini

*1 cup chopped red bell pepper (**about 1 medium**)*

*¹/₄ cup finely chopped onion (**about 1 small**)*

1 clove garlic, crushed

2 teaspoons olive or vegetable oil

*²/₃ cup shredded Swiss cheese (**about 2¹/₂ ounces**)*

¹/₄ cup chopped fresh or 1 tablespoon dried basil leaves

*1 can (**14 ounces**) artichoke hearts, drained and cut into fourths*

Mix cornmeal and cold water in 2-quart saucepan. Stir in boiling water and salt. Cook, stirring constantly, until mixture thickens and boils; reduce heat. Cover and cook 10 minutes, stirring occasionally. Add cheese and stir until smooth; keep polenta warm.

Cook squash, zucchini, bell pepper, onion and garlic in oil in 10-inch skillet over medium-high heat about 5 minutes, stirring occasionally, until vegetables are crisp-tender. Stir in basil and artichokes. Spoon polenta into shallow platter; top with vegetable mixture. *6 servings*

NUTRITION INFORMATION PER SERVING

ONE SERVING		PERCENT OF U.S. RDA	
Calories	190	Vitamin A	12%
Protein, g	8	Vitamin C	50%
Carbohydrate, g	31	Calcium	18%
Fat, g	6	Iron	12%
Unsaturated	3		
Saturated	3		
Dietary fiber, g	5		
Cholesterol, mg	10		
Sodium, mg	260		

Polenta with Italian Vegetables

Risotto Florentine

1 tablespoon margarine or butter

½ cup chopped onion (about 1 medium)

1 clove garlic, crushed

1 cup uncooked Arborio or other short grain rice

3 cups chicken broth or Vegetable Broth (page 14)

½ teaspoon saffron threads or ¼ teaspoon ground turmeric

1 can (15 to 16 ounces) cannellini beans, rinsed and drained

1 package (10 ounces) frozen chopped spinach, thawed and well drained

¼ cup grated Parmesan cheese

Heat margarine in 10-inch skillet over medium-high heat. Cook onion and garlic in margarine about 2 minutes, stirring occasionally, until onion is crisp-tender. Add rice; stir to coat with margarine mixture.

Stir in broth and saffron. Heat to boiling; stir once thoroughly and reduce heat. Cover and simmer 20 to 25 minutes or until rice is almost tender and liquid is absorbed. Stir in remaining ingredients. Cover and let stand 5 minutes. *4 servings*

NUTRITION INFORMATION PER SERVING

ONE SERVING		PERCENT OF U.S. RDA	
Calories	405	Vitamin A	42%
Protein, g	19	Vitamin C	14%
Carbohydrate, g	71	Calcium	20%
Fat, g	8	Iron	30%
Unsaturated	6		
Saturated	2		
Dietary fiber, g	7		
Cholesterol, mg	5		
Sodium, mg	970		

Mushroom Paprikàs

2 cups water

1 cup uncooked roasted buckwheat kernels (kasha)

1 tablespoon vegetable oil

1 cup chopped green onions (about 10 medium)

1 cup chopped green bell pepper

1 tablespoon sweet paprika

1 cup chicken broth or Vegetable Broth (page 14)

8 cups sliced mushrooms (about 2 pounds)

½ cup chopped fresh parsley

½ teaspoon salt

¼ teaspoon pepper

4 cups hot cooked noodles

½ cup nonfat or regular sour cream

Heat water and buckwheat kernels to boiling in 2-quart saucepan; reduce heat. Cover and simmer 18 to 20 minutes or until buckwheat is tender and liquid is absorbed.

Heat oil in 10-inch skillet over medium heat. Cook onions, bell pepper and paprika in oil 1 minute, stirring occasionally. Stir in broth and mushrooms. Cook about 5 minutes or until mushrooms are tender. Stir in buckwheat, parsley, salt and pepper. Serve over noodles. Top with sour cream. *4 servings*

NUTRITION INFORMATION PER SERVING

ONE SERVING		PERCENT OF U.S. RDA	
Calories	455	Vitamin A	18%
Protein, g	22	Vitamin C	50%
Carbohydrate, g	86	Calcium	16%
Fat, g	9	Iron	58%
Unsaturated	7		
Saturated	2		
Dietary fiber, g	14		
Cholesterol, mg	55		
Sodium, mg	770		

Barley-Vegetable Sauté

2 teaspoons margarine or butter

1 cup chopped onion (about 1 large)

1 cup chopped yellow bell pepper (about 1 medium)

1 clove garlic, crushed

4 cups cooked barley

2 tablespoons chopped fresh or 2 teaspoons dried thyme leaves

1/2 teaspoon salt

1 package (16 ounces) frozen whole kernel corn, thawed

1 package (10 ounces) frozen lima beans, thawed

Heat margarine in 10-inch skillet over medium-high heat. Cook onion, bell pepper and garlic in margarine about 2 minutes, stirring occasionally, until bell pepper is crisp-tender. Stir in remaining ingredients. Cook about 5 minutes, stirring occasionally, until hot. *4 servings*

NUTRITION INFORMATION PER SERVING

ONE SERVING		PERCENT OF U.S. RDA	
Calories	505	Vitamin A	8%
Protein, g	18	Vitamin C	40%
Carbohydrate, g	119	Calcium	6%
Fat, g	4	Iron	26%
Unsaturated	3		
Saturated	1		
Dietary fiber, g	20		
Cholesterol, mg	0		
Sodium, mg	350		

Quinoa and Bulgur Pilaf

1 cup uncooked quinoa

1 cup uncooked bulgur

3 1/2 cups chicken broth or Vegetable Broth (page 14)

1 tablespoon vegetable oil

1/2 cup chopped onion (about 1 medium)

2 cups chopped red cooking apples (about 2 medium)

1 cup dried apricots, cut up

1 cup dried prunes, cut up

1/2 cup chopped walnuts, toasted

1/2 teaspoon ground ginger

1/2 teaspoon ground cardamom

Heat quinoa, bulgur and broth to boiling in 2-quart saucepan; reduce heat. Cover and simmer 15 to 20 minutes or until liquid is absorbed.

Heat oil in 10-inch skillet over medium-high heat. Cook onion and apples in oil about 2 minutes, stirring occasionally, until crisp-tender. Stir in quinoa mixture and remaining ingredients. Cook about 5 minutes, stirring occasionally, until hot. *4 servings*

NUTRITION INFORMATION PER SERVING

ONE SERVING		PERCENT OF U.S. RDA	
Calories	695	Vitamin A	46%
Protein, g	21	Vitamin C	8%
Carbohydrate, g	124	Calcium	12%
Fat, g	18	Iron	44%
Unsaturated	15		
Saturated	3		
Dietary fiber, g	12		
Cholesterol, mg	0		
Sodium, mg	690		

Spiced Bulgur-and-Barley Balls

Grains replace a mixture of ground beef, pork and veal in this innovative revision of Swedish meatballs. Serve these "meatballs" over noodles with a light cream sauce for authentic Scandinavian flavor.

2¼ cups cooked bulgur
1½ cups cooked barley
¼ cup milk
2 tablespoons dry bread crumbs
½ teaspoon salt
¼ teaspoon ground nutmeg
¼ teaspoon ground allspice
1 egg, beaten
¼ cup ground walnuts
2 tablespoons margarine or butter

Mix all ingredients except walnuts and margarine. Shape into 1-inch balls. Roll balls in walnuts. Heat margarine in 10-inch skillet over medium-high heat. Cook balls in margarine 10 to 12 minutes, turning frequently, until light brown. Serve with cranberry sauce or lingonberry sauce if desired. *6 servings*

NUTRITION INFORMATION PER SERVING

ONE SERVING		PERCENT OF U.S. RDA	
Calories	200	Vitamin A	6%
Protein, g	6	Vitamin C	*
Carbohydrate, g	32	Calcium	4%
Fat, g	8	Iron	6%
Unsaturated	6		
Saturated	2		
Dietary fiber, g	6		
Cholesterol, mg	35		
Sodium, mg	950		

Noodles Romanoff

8 ounces uncooked wide egg noodles
2 cups low-fat or regular sour cream
¼ cup grated Parmesan cheese
1 tablespoon chopped fresh chives
1 teaspoon salt
⅛ teaspoon pepper
1 large clove garlic, crushed
2 tablespoons margarine or butter
¼ cup grated Parmesan cheese

Cook noodles as directed on package; drain. Mix sour cream, ¼ cup cheese, the chives, salt, pepper and garlic. Stir margarine into hot noodles. Fold in sour cream mixture. Arrange noodles on warm platter. Sprinkle with ¼ cup cheese. Serve immediately. *6 servings*

NUTRITION INFORMATION PER SERVING

ONE SERVING		PERCENT OF U.S. RDA	
Calories	305	Vitamin A	18%
Protein, g	13	Vitamin C	*
Carbohydrate, g	36	Calcium	20%
Fat, g	13	Iron	10%
Unsaturated	5		
Saturated	8		
Dietary fiber, g	2		
Cholesterol, mg	75		
Sodium, mg	750		

Double Spinach Fettuccine

To add protein when serving this for a meal, offer low-fat frozen yogurt or ice milk and assorted toppings for dessert.

8 ounces spinach fettuccine

1 teaspoon vegetable oil

1 clove garlic, crushed

3 cups shredded spinach (about 4 ounces)

1¼ cups thinly sliced zucchini (about 2 small)

¼ cup unsalted sunflower nuts, toasted

2 tablespoons grated lemon peel

½ teaspoon salt

1 can (15 to 16 ounces) garbanzo beans, rinsed and drained

Cook fettuccine as directed on package; drain. Heat oil in 10-inch skillet over medium-high heat. Cook garlic in oil, stirring occasionally, until golden. Stir in remaining ingredients. Cook about 2 minutes, stirring occasionally, until zucchini is tender. Stir in fettuccine. *4 servings*

NUTRITION INFORMATION PER SERVING

ONE SERVING		PERCENT OF U.S. RDA	
Calories	256	Vitamin A	30%
Protein, g	12	Vitamin C	16%
Carbohydrate, g	40	Calcium	12%
Fat, g	8	Iron	24%
Unsaturated	7		
Saturated	1		
Dietary fiber, g	7		
Cholesterol, mg	20		
Sodium, mg	570		

Angel Hair Patties

1 package (8 ounces) angel hair pasta

1 teaspoon olive or vegetable oil

2 cups julienne strips carrots (about 4 medium)

1 tablespoon chopped fresh or 1 teaspoon dried basil leaves

¼ teaspoon salt

1 package (10 ounces) frozen chopped spinach, thawed and well drained

½ cup Egg Substitute (page 88) or cholesterol-free egg product or 2 eggs

½ cup low-fat or regular ricotta cheese

¼ cup grated Parmesan cheese

¼ teaspoon pepper

1 teaspoon olive or vegetable oil

2 cups spaghetti sauce, heated

Cook pasta as directed on package. Meanwhile, heat 1 teaspoon oil in 10-inch skillet over medium heat. Cook carrots, basil, salt and spinach in oil about 2 minutes, stirring occasionally, until carrots are crisp-tender. Remove vegetable mixture from skillet; keep warm.

Drain pasta. Mix pasta, Egg Substitute, cheeses and pepper. Shape into patties, each 1 inch thick. Heat 1 teaspoon oil in skillet over medium-high heat. Cook patties in oil 6 to 8 minutes, turning after 4 minutes, until golden brown. Top patties with vegetable mixture and spaghetti sauce. *4 servings*

NUTRITION INFORMATION PER SERVING

ONE SERVING		PERCENT OF U.S. RDA	
Calories	425	Vitamin A	100%
Protein, g	20	Vitamin C	22%
Carbohydrate, g	70	Calcium	32%
Fat, g	11	Iron	28%
Unsaturated	8		
Saturated	3		
Dietary fiber, g	8		
Cholesterol, mg	15		
Sodium, mg	1460		

Sicilian Fusilli

*1 package (12 ounces) tricolored
corkscrew (fusilli) pasta*

1 tablespoon olive or vegetable oil

*1 tablespoon chopped fresh or 1 teaspoon
dried basil leaves*

1 teaspoon freshly ground pepper

*2 cups julienne strips carrots (about 4
medium)*

*1 medium yellow bell pepper, cut into
2-inch strips*

*1 can (15 to 16 ounces) cannellini beans,
rinsed and drained*

*1 can (15 ounces) tomato sauce with
tomato bits*

*1 can (14 ounces) artichoke hearts,
drained and cut into fourths*

*¹/₂ cup freshly grated Parmesan cheese or
shredded farmer cheese*

Cook pasta as directed on package; drain. Heat oil
in 12-inch skillet over medium-high heat. Cook
basil, pepper, carrots and bell pepper in oil about
3 minutes, stirring occasionally, until carrots are
crisp-tender. Stir in pasta, beans, tomato sauce
and artichoke hearts. Cook about 5 minutes, stirring occasionally, until hot. Sprinkle with cheese.
6 servings

NUTRITION INFORMATION PER SERVING

ONE SERVING		PERCENT OF U.S. RDA	
Calories	480	Vitamin A	100%
Protein, g	20	Vitamin C	20%
Carbohydrate, g	90	Calcium	18%
Fat, g	8	Iron	34%
Unsaturated	6		
Saturated	2		
Dietary fiber, g	8		
Cholesterol, mg	5		
Sodium, mg	1130		

Sicilian Fusilli

Spaghetti and Spicy Rice Balls

2 cups cooked regular long grain rice

¹/₂ cup quick-cooking oats

*¹/₂ cup finely chopped onion (about 1
medium)*

¹/₄ cup dry bread crumbs

¹/₄ cup milk

*1 tablespoon chopped fresh or 1 teaspoon
dried basil leaves*

*2 teaspoons chopped fresh or ¹/₂ teaspoon
dried oregano leaves*

¹/₄ teaspoon ground red pepper (cayenne)

1 egg, beaten

¹/₂ cup wheat germ

1 tablespoon vegetable oil

4 cups hot cooked spaghetti

2 cups spaghetti sauce, heated

Mix rice, oats, onion, bread crumbs, milk, basil,
oregano, red pepper and egg. Shape into 10 balls.
Roll balls in wheat germ. Heat oil in 10-inch
skillet over medium heat. Cook balls in oil about
10 minutes, turning occasionally, until light
golden brown. Serve on spaghetti. Top with spaghetti sauce. *5 servings*

NUTRITION INFORMATION PER SERVING

ONE SERVING		PERCENT OF U.S. RDA	
Calories	445	Vitamin A	8%
Protein, g	16	Vitamin C	10%
Carbohydrate, g	81	Calcium	10%
Fat, g	11	Iron	28%
Unsaturated	9		
Saturated	2		
Dietary fiber, g	7		
Cholesterol, mg	45		
Sodium, mg	1180		

Swedish Summer Hash

Dill is a very popular herb in Scandinavian kitchens and sparks fresh flavor in this vegetable hash.

1 tablespoon margarine or butter

3/4 cup chopped yellow bell pepper (about 1 medium)

1/4 cup chopped green onions

2 tablespoons chopped fresh chives

1 1/2 cups Egg Substitute (page 88) or cholesterol-free egg product or 6 eggs

1 tablespoon chopped fresh or 1 teaspoon dried dill weed

3/4 pound new potatoes, cooked and cut into fourths

1 package (10 ounces) frozen green peas, thawed

1 cup chopped seeded tomato (about 1 large)

1/2 cup plain nonfat or regular yogurt

1/2 cup shredded farmer cheese (2 ounces)

Heat margarine in 10-inch skillet over medium heat. Cook bell pepper, onions and chives in margarine about 2 minutes, stirring occasionally, until bell pepper is crisp-tender. Stir in Egg Substitute and dill weed. Cook 3 to 4 minutes, stirring occasionally, until eggs are thickened throughout but still moist. Stir in potatoes and peas. Cook until hot. Top hash with tomato, yogurt and cheese. *4 servings*

NUTRITION INFORMATION PER SERVING

ONE SERVING		PERCENT OF U.S. RDA	
Calories	265	Vitamin A	24%
Protein, g	19	Vitamin C	50%
Carbohydrate, g	35	Calcium	26%
Fat, g	8	Iron	24%
Unsaturated	5		
Saturated	3		
Dietary fiber, g	6		
Cholesterol, mg	15		
Sodium, mg	390		

Swedish Summer Hash

Stuffed Chiles with Walnut Sauce

8 whole Anaheim or poblano chiles

3 cups shredded part-skim mozzarella cheese (12 ounces)

1 cup nonfat cream cheese product or 1 package (8 ounces) cream cheese, softened

¹/₂ cup Egg Substitute (page 88) or cholesterol-free egg product or 2 eggs

2 teaspoons vegetable oil

¹/₂ cup low-fat or regular ricotta cheese

¹/₄ cup ground walnuts

¹/₄ cup milk

1 teaspoon sugar

Dash of ground cinnamon

Set oven control to broil. Carefully cut 1 slit in each chile from top to bottom and remove seeds, leaving stem intact. Broil chiles about 4 inches from heat 10 minutes, turning after 5 minutes, until chiles begin to blister.

Mix mozzarella cheese, cream cheese product and Egg Substitute. Fill each chile with about ¹/₃ cup cheese mixture. Heat oil in 10-inch skillet over low heat. Place chiles in skillet. Cover and cook 15 to 20 minutes or until filling is hot. Mix remaining ingredients until smooth. Serve with chiles. *4 servings*

NUTRITION INFORMATION PER SERVING

ONE SERVING		PERCENT OF U.S. RDA	
Calories	275	Vitamin A	94%
Protein, g	25	Vitamin C	100%
Carbohydrate, g	11	Calcium	62%
Fat, g	15	Iron	6%
Unsaturated	6		
Saturated	9		
Dietary fiber, g	1		
Cholesterol, mg	45		
Sodium, mg	450		

Layered Eggplant Parmigiana

2 cups water

1 cup uncooked bulgur

³/₄ cup Egg Substitute (page 88) or cholesterol-free egg product or 3 eggs

³/₄ cup Italian-style dry bread crumbs

¹/₄ cup chopped fresh parsley

¹/₄ cup grated Parmesan cheese

1 tablespoon chopped fresh or 1 teaspoon dried basil leaves

1 tablespoon olive or vegetable oil

1 small eggplant (about 1 pound), thinly sliced

1 can (8 ounces) tomato sauce

¹/₂ cup shredded part-skim mozzarella cheese (2 ounces)

Heat water to boiling in 2-quart saucepan; remove from heat and stir in bulgur. Let stand uncovered 30 to 60 minutes or until liquid is absorbed. Mix bulgur, Egg Substitute, bread crumbs, parsley, Parmesan cheese and basil.

Heat oil in 10-inch skillet over low heat. Place half of the eggplant slices in skillet; top with bulgur mixture. Arrange remaining eggplant slices over bulgur; top with tomato sauce. Cover and cook 30 to 35 minutes or until eggplant is tender. Sprinkle with mozzarella cheese. *6 servings*

NUTRITION INFORMATION PER SERVING

ONE SERVING		PERCENT OF U.S. RDA	
Calories	260	Vitamin A	8%
Protein, g	14	Vitamin C	16%
Carbohydrate, g	46	Calcium	18%
Fat, g	6	Iron	14%
Unsaturated	4		
Saturated	2		
Dietary fiber, g	9		
Cholesterol, mg	10		
Sodium, mg	500		

Root Vegetables with Citrus Sauce

A crisp fall day is the perfect time to indulge in this contemporary version of comfort food. Served with hard rolls, a mixed green salad and creamy bread pudding for dessert, this will warm up anyone's appetite.

1 tablespoon margarine or butter

4 ounces pearl onions, peeled and cut into halves

³/₄ cup whole baby carrots (about 4 ounces)

1 small parsnip, peeled and cut into 2-inch pieces (about 1 cup)

1 medium sweet potato, peeled and cut into 2-inch pieces

2 tablespoons grated orange peel

1 cup orange juice

¹/₂ cup chicken broth or Vegetable Broth (page 14)

1 tablespoon chopped fresh or 1 teaspoon dried thyme leaves

¹/₄ teaspoon salt

4 cups hot cooked brown rice

Heat margarine in 10-inch skillet over medium heat. Cook onions, carrots, parsnip and sweet potato in margarine 2 to 3 minutes, stirring occasionally, until vegetables are golden brown. Stir in remaining ingredients except rice; reduce heat. Cover and simmer 20 to 25 minutes or until vegetables are tender. Serve with rice. *4 servings*

NUTRITION INFORMATION PER SERVING

ONE SERVING		PERCENT OF U.S. RDA	
Calories	330	Vitamin A	100%
Protein, g	7	Vitamin C	50%
Carbohydrate, g	71	Calcium	60%
Fat, g	5	Iron	10%
Unsaturated	4		
Saturated	1		
Dietary fiber, g	7		
Cholesterol, mg	0		
Sodium, mg	840		

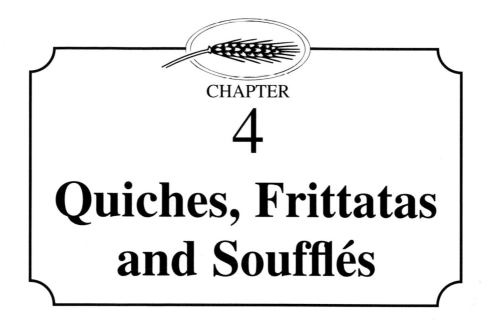

CHAPTER

4

Quiches, Frittatas and Soufflés

This chapter is for everyone, even those who are watching their cholesterol! You'll find our Egg Substitute (page 88) is a great way to enjoy egg dishes that used to be "off limits." We have also kept a careful eye on fat, suggesting reduced-fat cheeses and other dairy products when necessary, to keep this scrumptious chapter truly guilt free. So, go ahead, and dig into a luscious Rice and Bean Quiche, Mexican Strata or an Egg Burrito Grande and enjoy every bit of your meal!

Garden Phyllo Quiches (page 90)

Egg Substitute

Cholesterol watchers will appreciate the economy of this homemade version of egg substitute. For even color, combine egg and food color well before adding the oil. One large egg equals about ¼ cup of egg substitute. Use the ½-cup recipe below for 2 whole eggs or ½-cup cholesterol-free egg product. Cover and refrigerate this Egg Substitute no longer than 2 days.

FOR ½ CUP

3 egg whites

3 drops yellow food color

1 teaspoon vegetable oil

FOR 1 CUP

6 egg whites

6 drops yellow food color

2 teaspoons vegetable oil

Mix egg whites and food color. Mix in oil. Cover and refrigerate up to 2 days. *2 or 4 servings (about ¼ cup each)*

NUTRITION INFORMATION PER SERVING

ONE SERVING		PERCENT OF U.S. RDA	
Calories	40	Vitamin A	*
Protein, g	5	Vitamin C	*
Carbohydrate, g	1	Calcium	*
Fat, g	2	Iron	*
Unsaturated	2		
Saturated	0		
Dietary fiber, g	0		
Cholesterol, mg	0		
Sodium, mg	80		

Rice and Bean Quiche

1½ cups cooked brown or regular long grain rice

¼ cup chopped fresh parsley

1½ cups Egg Substitute (left) or cholesterol-free egg product or 6 eggs

1½ cups cooked dried black beans or 1 can (15 ounces) black beans, rinsed and drained

1 teaspoon chile powder

¼ teaspoon salt

¼ teaspoon pepper

1 can (4 ounces) chopped green chiles, drained

¾ cup chopped seeded tomato (about 1 medium)

½ cup shredded reduced-fat or regular Cheddar cheese (2 ounces)

Heat oven to 350°. Spray pie plate, 9×1¼ inches, with nonstick cooking spray. Mix rice, parsley and ¼ cup of the Egg Substitute in pie plate. Press rice mixture on bottom and up side of pie plate. Bake 5 minutes.

Spread beans over rice crust. Mix remaining 1¼ cups Egg Substitute, the chile powder, salt, pepper and chiles; pour over beans. Bake 20 to 30 minutes or until knife inserted in center comes out clean. Top with tomato and cheese. Let stand 5 minutes. *6 servings*

NUTRITION INFORMATION PER SERVING

ONE SERVING		PERCENT OF U.S. RDA	
Calories	170	Vitamin A	10%
Protein, g	14	Vitamin C	34%
Carbohydrate, g	27	Calcium	14%
Fat, g	3	Iron	14%
Unsaturated	2		
Saturated	1		
Dietary fiber, g	5		
Cholesterol, mg	5		
Sodium, mg	620		

Rice and Bean Quiche

Garden Phyllo Quiches

1 package (10 ounces) frozen chopped spinach, thawed and well drained

1 cup sliced mushrooms (about 3 ounces)

1 cup milk

1/2 teaspoon ground mustard

1/4 teaspoon salt

1/8 teaspoon ground nutmeg

2 eggs

4 frozen phyllo sheets, thawed

2 teaspoons margarine or butter, melted

1/4 cup shredded part-skim mozzarella cheese (1 ounce)

1/4 cup alfalfa sprouts

Heat oven to 350°. Spray 10-inch skillet with nonstick cooking spray. Cook spinach and mushrooms in skillet over medium heat, stirring occasionally, until spinach is wilted and mushrooms are tender. Remove from heat. Mix milk, mustard, salt, nutmeg and eggs; reserve.

Spray four 6-ounce custard cups with nonstick cooking spray. Place 1 phyllo sheet on flat surface; lightly brush with margarine. Top with second phyllo sheet; brush with margarine. Continue with remaining phyllo sheets and margarine. Cut phyllo into fourths. Place 1 phyllo section in each custard cup. Trim overhanging edge of phyllo 1 inch from rim of cup.

Divide spinach mixture evenly among cups. Pour about 1/3 cup egg mixture into each cup. Fold edges of phyllo toward center. Bake 15 to 20 minutes or until egg mixture is set. Sprinkle with cheese. Top with alfalfa sprouts. Serve immediately. *4 servings*

NUTRITION INFORMATION PER SERVING

ONE SERVING		PERCENT OF U.S. RDA	
Calories	250	Vitamin A	50%
Protein, g	11	Vitamin C	14%
Carbohydrate, g	22	Calcium	20%
Fat, g	7	Iron	14%
Unsaturated	4		
Saturated	3		
Dietary fiber, g	2		
Cholesterol, mg	115		
Sodium, mg	370		

Broccoli and Swiss Cheese Frittata

1/2 cup chopped onion (about 1 medium)

2 cloves garlic, finely chopped

2 tablespoons margarine or butter

1 tablespoon olive or vegetable oil

1 package (10 ounces) frozen chopped broccoli, thawed and drained

8 eggs

1/2 teaspoon salt

1/4 teaspoon pepper

1 cup shredded Swiss cheese (4 ounces)

1 to 2 tablespoons chopped fresh or 1 teaspoon dried oregano leaves

2 tablespoons shredded Swiss cheese

Cook onion and garlic in margarine and oil in 10-inch ovenproof skillet over medium heat about 5 minutes, stirring occasionally, until onion is crisp-tender; remove from heat. Stir in broccoli. Beat eggs, salt and pepper until blended. Stir 1 cup cheese and the oregano into eggs; pour over broccoli mixture. Cover and cook over medium-low heat 9 to 11 minutes or until eggs are set around edge and light brown on bottom. Remove cover.

Set oven control to broil. Broil frittata with top about 5 inches from heat about 2 minutes or until golden brown. Sprinkle with 2 tablespoons cheese. Cut into wedges. *6 servings*

NUTRITION INFORMATION PER SERVING

ONE SERVING		PERCENT OF U.S. RDA	
Calories	240	Vitamin A	25%
Protein, g	16	Vitamin C	30%
Carbohydrate, g	6	Calcium	26%
Fat, g	18	Iron	8%
Unsaturated	11		
Saturated	7		
Dietary fiber, g	2		
Cholesterol, mg	300		
Sodium, mg	370		

Spinach Frittata with Creole Sauce

Toasted slices of Cinnamon-Nut Batter Bread (page 133) and cut-up fresh fruit make a delicious accompaniment to this frittata inspired by the flavors of New Orleans.

Creole Sauce (right)

¹/₄ cup chopped onion (about 1 small)

2 teaspoons margarine or butter

3 cups coarsely chopped spinach (about 4 ounces)

1¹/₂ cups Egg Substitute (page 88) or cholesterol-free egg product or 6 eggs

¹/₂ teaspoon chopped fresh or ¹/₈ teaspoon dried thyme leaves

¹/₈ teaspoon salt

¹/₈ teaspoon pepper

2 tablespoons shredded part-skim or regular mozzarella cheese

Prepare Creole Sauce; keep warm. Cook onion in margarine in 10-inch nonstick skillet over medium heat 3 minutes, stirring occasionally. Add spinach; toss just until spinach is wilted.

Beat Egg Substitute, thyme, salt and pepper; pour over spinach. Cover and cook over medium-low heat 5 to 7 minutes or until eggs are set and light brown on bottom. Sprinkle with cheese. Cut into wedges. Serve with Creole Sauce. *4 servings*

CREOLE SAUCE

1 cup coarsely chopped tomato (about 1 large)

¹/₄ cup chopped onion (about 1 small)

2 tablespoons sliced celery

¹/₄ teaspoon paprika

¹/₈ teaspoon pepper

4 drops red pepper sauce

Heat all ingredients to boiling in 1-quart saucepan, stirring occasionally; reduce heat. Simmer uncovered about 5 minutes, stirring occasionally, until thickened.

NUTRITION INFORMATION PER SERVING

ONE SERVING		PERCENT OF U.S. RDA	
Calories	105	Vitamin A	70%
Protein, g	12	Vitamin C	34%
Carbohydrate, g	11	Calcium	20%
Fat, g	3	Iron	16%
Unsaturated	2		
Saturated	1		
Dietary fiber, g	3		
Cholesterol, mg	5		
Sodium, mg	360		

Southwestern Frittata

Serving Calico Corn Muffins (page 132) will add a further touch of southwestern flavor to this festive quiche.

1/2 cup chopped onion (about 1 medium)

6 eggs

1/2 cup milk

1/2 teaspoon chile powder

1/4 teaspoon dried oregano leaves

1 can (11 ounces) whole kernel corn with red and green peppers, drained

1/4 cup shredded Cheddar cheese (1 ounce)

1/2 cup salsa

Spray 10-inch skillet with nonstick cooking spray. Cook onion in skillet over medium heat, stirring occasionally, until tender. Beat eggs, milk, chile powder and oregano until well mixed; pour over onion. Stir in corn. Cover and cook over medium-low heat 9 to 11 minutes or until eggs are set around edge and light brown on bottom. Sprinkle with cheese. Cut into wedges. Serve with salsa. *6 servings*

NUTRITION INFORMATION PER SERVING

ONE SERVING		PERCENT OF U.S. RDA	
Calories	145	Vitamin A	10%
Protein, g	9	Vitamin C	8%
Carbohydrate, g	12	Calcium	10%
Fat, g	7	Iron	8%
Unsaturated	4		
Saturated	3		
Dietary fiber, g	1		
Cholesterol, mg	220		
Sodium, mg	430		

Southwestern Frittata, Cinnamon-Nut Batter Bread (page 133)

Blue Cheese Omelet with Pears

4 eggs

2 teaspoons margarine or butter

2 tablespoons crumbled Danish blue cheese or Gorgonzola cheese

1 tablespoon chopped fresh chives

1 pear, cut into wedges

Mix eggs just until whites and yolks are blended. Heat margarine in 8-inch skillet or omelet pan over medium-high heat just until margarine begins to brown. As margarine melts, tilt skillet to coat bottom completely.

Quickly pour eggs, all at once, into skillet. Slide skillet back and forth rapidly over heat and, at the same time, quickly stir with fork to spread eggs continuously over bottom of skillet as they thicken. Let stand over heat a few seconds to lightly brown bottom of omelet. (Do not overcook—omelet will continue to cook after folding.)

Tilt skillet; run fork under edge of omelet, then jerk skillet sharply to loosen omelet from bottom of skillet. Sprinkle with cheese and chives. Fold portion of omelet nearest you just to center. (Allow for portion of omelet to slide up side of skillet.) Grasp skillet handle; turn omelet onto warm plate, flipping folded portion of omelet over so far side is on bottom. Serve with pear wedges. *2 servings*

NUTRITION INFORMATION PER SERVING

ONE SERVING		PERCENT OF U.S. RDA	
Calories	255	Vitamin A	22%
Protein, g	14	Vitamin C	6%
Carbohydrate, g	14	Calcium	10%
Fat, g	17	Iron	8%
Unsaturated	11		
Saturated	6		
Dietary fiber, g	3		
Cholesterol, mg	430		
Sodium, mg	290		

Beating the Clock

Everyone wants delicious breakfasts, lunches and dinners that can be on the table in no time. In addition to the recipes listed here, all of which can be prepared in half an hour or less, you'll find other ideas to solve the time crunch of meal preparation easily.

• Stock your pantry and refrigerator with items you use frequently, such as rice, pasta, canned beans, tomato sauce, chicken broth, vegetable broth, onions, garlic and dry bread crumbs. Other items that are handy to include are cheeses, cut-up fresh vegetables, eggs and cholesterol-free egg products, milk and bread.

• Read the recipe completely and assemble all the ingredients and equipment you'll need before starting to cook.

• Use the correct utensils and equipment for each task.

• Always keep knives sharp; cutting will be faster and safer.

• When cooking rice, pasta, beans or legumes, double the amount and save half for use in future recipes. Cooked rice can be covered and frozen for 6 months or refrigerated as long as a week. Cooked pasta can be tossed with a small amount of oil and stored, covered, up to 2 days in the refrigerator. Beans and legumes can be covered and frozen for up to 6 months or refrigerated up to 5 days. These ingredients can all be reheated in the microwave or on top of the stove. Pasta can be reheated by placing in boiling water just until hot.

• When you have time, prepare such staples as toasted coconut, toasted nuts, and dry and fresh bread crumbs. Cover tightly and store for future use.

• Purchase cut-up vegetables from your deli, salad bar or produce departments. You can also cut up your own vegetables ahead of time.

• Get family and friends involved by assigning them some preparation and cooking tasks.

30-Minute Menus

SOUPS, STEWS AND CHILE

Bean and Pepper Chile (page 25)
Cabbage-Bean Soup with Rivels (page 9)
Caribbean Stew with Pineapple Salsa (page 22)
Curried Stew with Peanut Sauce (page 20)
Green Jerked Chile (page 28)
Pizza Soup (page 4)
Santa Fe Corn Chowder (page 2)
Vegetable Stew with Dill Dumplings (page 21)

EASY SKILLETS AND STIR-FRIES

Barley-Vegetable Sauté (page 77)
Black Bean Enchiladas (page 61)
Double Spinach Fettuccine (page 79)
Vegetable Sauté with Black Beans and Couscous (page 63)

QUICHES, FRITTATAS AND SOUFFLÉS

Egg Burrito Grande (page 97)
Vegetable Poached Eggs (page 101)

SATISFYING SALADS

Vegetable-Couscous Salad (page 112)
Black Bean Taco Salad (page 104)
Southwestern Wild Rice Salad (page 112)

PIZZA, SANDWICHES AND BREADS

Four-Cheese Pesto Pizza (page 123)
Fruited Gorgonzola and Cheddar Melts (page 124)
Italian Grinders (page 127)
Meatless "Meatball" Pizza (page 122)
Mediterranean Pizza (page 122)
Mexican Pita Tostadas (page 127)

Rolled Cheese Soufflé

This creative soufflé is rolled like a jelly roll and contains a cheese filling dotted with sun-dried tomatoes.

¹/₄ cup (¹/₂ stick) margarine or butter

¹/₄ cup all-purpose flour

¹/₄ teaspoon salt

1¹/₂ cups milk

5 eggs, separated

¹/₂ teaspoon cream of tartar

Cheesy Tomato Filling (right)

Heat oven to 350°. Spray bottom only of jelly roll pan, 15¹/₂×10¹/₂×1 inch, with nonstick cooking spray. Line bottom of pan with waxed paper or cooking parchment paper; spray with nonstick cooking spray. Heat margarine in 2-quart saucepan over low heat until melted. Stir in flour and salt. Cook, stirring constantly, until smooth and bubbly; remove from heat. Gradually stir in milk. Heat to boiling, stirring constantly. Boil and stir 1 minute; remove from heat. Beat in egg yolks, one at a time.

Beat egg whites and cream of tartar in large bowl on high speed until stiff but not dry. Stir about one-fourth of the egg whites into egg yolk mixture. Fold egg yolk mixture into remaining egg whites. Spread evenly in pan. Bake 25 to 30 minutes or until puffed and golden brown. Meanwhile, prepare Cheesy Tomato Filling. Immediately loosen soufflé from edges of pan; invert onto cloth-covered wire rack. Carefully peel off waxed paper. Spread filling over soufflé. Roll up soufflé, beginning at narrow end. Cut into slices. Serve immediately. *5 servings*

CHEESY TOMATO FILLING

¹/₂ cup sun-dried tomatoes (not oil-packed)

¹/₂ cup drained chopped seeded tomato (about 1 small)

¹/₂ cup finely chopped fresh parsley

³/₄ cup low-fat or regular ricotta cheese

2 tablespoons chopped fresh parsley

1 tablespoon chopped fresh or 1 teaspoon dried thyme leaves

Pour enough hot water over sun-dried tomatoes to cover. Let stand 10 to 15 minutes or until softened; drain and chop. Spray 10-inch skillet with nonstick cooking spray. Heat sun-dried tomatoes, chopped seeded tomato and parsley in skillet, stirring occasionally, until hot; remove from heat. Stir in remaining ingredients. Heat over low heat, stirring constantly.

NUTRITION INFORMATION PER SERVING

ONE SERVING		PERCENT OF U.S. RDA	
Calories	305	Vitamin A	46%
Protein, g	15	Vitamin C	90%
Carbohydrate, g	20	Calcium	24%
Fat, g	19	Iron	16%
Unsaturated	13		
Saturated	6		
Dietary fiber, g	2		
Cholesterol, mg	230		
Sodium, mg	380		

Mexican Strata

8 slices whole grain bread

1¹/₂ cups shredded reduced-fat or regular Cheddar cheese (6 ounces)

1 can (4 ounces) chopped green chiles, well drained

1 jar (2 ounces) sliced pimientos, well drained

1¹/₃ cups milk

1 cup Egg Substitute (page 88) or cholesterol-free egg product or 4 eggs

¹/₄ teaspoon ground cumin

Spray square baking dish, 8×8×2 inches with nonstick cooking spray. Remove crusts from bread. Place 4 slices bread in baking dish. Sprinkle with cheese, chiles and pimientos. Top with remaining bread. Beat remaining ingredients; pour over bread. Cover and refrigerate at least 2 hours but no longer than 24 hours.

Heat oven to 325°. Bake 1 to 1¹/₄ hours or until set and top is golden brown. Let stand 10 minutes before serving. *4 servings*

NUTRITION INFORMATION PER SERVING

ONE SERVING		PERCENT OF U.S. RDA	
Calories	315	Vitamin A	16%
Protein, g	26	Vitamin C	50%
Carbohydrate, g	35	Calcium	46%
Fat, g	9	Iron	12%
Unsaturated	4		
Saturated	5		
Dietary fiber, g	3		
Cholesterol, mg	25		
Sodium, mg	940		

Asian Omelet

6 eggs

¹/₂ cup milk

¹/₂ teaspoon pepper

1 teaspoon vegetable oil

1 cup cooked brown or regular long grain rice

1 tablespoon finely chopped carrot

1 tablespoon finely chopped green bell pepper

1 tablespoon finely chopped red bell pepper

1 tablespoon finely chopped green onion

1 tablespoon finely chopped mushrooms

1 clove garlic, finely chopped

1 tablespoon soy sauce

Beat eggs, milk and pepper slightly; reserve. Heat oil in 8-inch nonstick skillet or omelet pan over medium-high heat. Cook remaining ingredients except soy sauce in oil, stirring frequently, until vegetables are crisp-tender. Stir in soy sauce. Remove from skillet; keep warm.

Spray same skillet with nonstick cooking spray. Heat skillet over medium-high heat. Quickly pour about ¹/₂ cup of the egg mixture into skillet. Slide skillet back and forth rapidly over heat and, at the same time, quickly stir with fork to spread eggs continuously over bottom of skillet as they thicken. Let stand over heat a few seconds to lightly brown bottom of omelet. (Do not overcook—omelet will continue to cook after folding.)

Spoon about ¹/₄ cup of the rice mixture on one side of omelet. Run spatula under unfilled side of omelet; lift over rice mixture. Tilting skillet slightly, turn omelet onto plate. Repeat with remaining egg and rice mixtures. *4 servings*

NUTRITION INFORMATION PER SERVING

ONE SERVING		PERCENT OF U.S. RDA	
Calories	195	Vitamin A	20%
Protein, g	12	Vitamin C	10%
Carbohydrate, g	15	Calcium	10%
Fat, g	10	Iron	10%
Unsaturated	7		
Saturated	3		
Dietary fiber, g	1		
Cholesterol, mg	320		
Sodium, mg	510		

Egg Burrito Grande

Traditional refried beans are prepared with lard, but the vegetarian product used here is prepared with vegetable oil.

*1 cup diced potato (**about 1 medium**)*

*1 cup chopped green bell pepper (**about 1 medium**)*

*¼ cup chopped onion (**about 1 small**)*

½ teaspoon chile powder

1 teaspoon margarine or butter

5 eggs, slightly beaten

1 cup canned vegetarian refried beans, heated

*½ cup shredded reduced-fat or regular Cheddar cheese (**2 ounces**)*

*½ cup chopped seeded tomato (**about 1 small**)*

½ cup salsa

*8 flour tortillas (**8 to 10 inches in diameter**)*

Spray 10-inch skillet with nonstick cooking spray. Cook potato, bell pepper and onion in skillet over medium heat, stirring occasionally, until tender. Stir in chile powder. Remove from skillet; keep warm.

Heat margarine in same skillet over medium heat until melted. Cook eggs in margarine, stirring frequently, until set but still moist. For each burrito, spread about 2 tablespoons beans, 2 tablespoons potato mixture, 1 tablespoon cheese, 2 tablespoons eggs, 1 tablespoon tomato and 1 tablespoon salsa in center of each tortilla. Fold tortilla around filling. *4 servings*

NUTRITION INFORMATION PER SERVING

ONE SERVING		PERCENT OF U.S. RDA	
Calories	510	Vitamin A	20%
Protein, g	23	Vitamin C	46%
Carbohydrate, g	73	Calcium	22%
Fat, g	17	Iron	32%
Unsaturated	10		
Saturated	7		
Dietary fiber, g	7		
Cholesterol, mg	280		
Sodium, mg	1070		

Using Egg Whites

Healthful eating doesn't mean you have to give up eggs or your favorite recipes made with eggs. By using whole eggs in moderation or by using egg substitutes, you can still eat many of your favorite dishes. Use the chart below to substitute egg whites for whole eggs, or use ¼ cup Egg Substitute or purchased cholesterol-free egg product for each whole egg. Some brands of cholesterol-free egg product contain fat while others do not; read package labels to choose the brand that meets your needs.

Instead of	Use
1 egg	2 egg whites
2 eggs	3 egg whites
3 eggs	5 egg whites
4 eggs	6 egg whites

Easy Oven Pancake

1 tablespoon margarine or butter

4 eggs

½ cup all-purpose flour

½ cup whole wheat flour

1 cup milk

¼ teaspoon salt

¼ teaspoon onion powder

2 cups broccoli flowerets

1 cup sliced mushrooms (about 3 ounces)

1 cup marinara or spaghetti sauce

⅓ cup shredded Cheddar cheese

2 tablespoons sunflower nuts

Heat oven to 425°. Heat margarine in pie plate, 9×1¼ inches, in oven until melted. Beat eggs with hand beater or wire whisk until fluffy. Beat in flours, milk, salt and onion powder just until smooth. Pour into pie plate. Bake 20 to 25 minutes or until puffed and golden brown.

Meanwhile, spray 10-inch skillet with nonstick cooking spray. Cook broccoli and mushrooms in skillet, stirring occasionally, until broccoli is crisp-tender. Stir in marinara sauce; heat through. Top pancake with vegetable mixture. Sprinkle with cheese and nuts. *6 servings*

NUTRITION INFORMATION PER SERVING

ONE SERVING		PERCENT OF U.S. RDA	
Calories	235	Vitamin A	26%
Protein, g	13	Vitamin C	54%
Carbohydrate, g	26	Calcium	14%
Fat, g	11	Iron	14%
Unsaturated	7		
Saturated	4		
Dietary fiber, g	5		
Cholesterol, mg	150		
Sodium, mg	420		

Tex-Mex Scrambled Eggs

2 teaspoons vegetable oil

3 corn tortillas (about 6 inches in diameter), cut into thin strips

¼ cup chopped onion (about 1 small)

2 cups Egg Substitute (page 88) or cholesterol-free egg product or 8 eggs

½ jalapeño chile, seeded and chopped

1 cup salsa

¼ cup low-fat or regular sour cream

2 tablespoons chopped green onions

Heat oil in 10-inch nonstick skillet over medium-high heat. Cook tortillas and ¼ cup onion in oil about 5 minutes, stirring frequently, until tortillas are crisp. Mix Egg Substitute and chile. Pour over tortilla mixture; reduce heat to medium.

As mixture begins to set at bottom and side, gently lift cooked portions with spatula so that thin, uncooked portion can flow to bottom. Do not stir. Cook 4 to 5 minutes or until eggs are set but still moist. Top each serving with salsa, sour cream and green onions. *4 servings*

NUTRITION INFORMATION PER SERVING

ONE SERVING		PERCENT OF U.S. RDA	
Calories	160	Vitamin A	20%
Protein, g	14	Vitamin C	24%
Carbohydrate, g	19	Calcium	14%
Fat, g	4	Iron	16%
Unsaturated	3		
Saturated	1		
Dietary fiber, g	2		
Cholesterol, mg	5		
Sodium, mg	910		

Easy Oven Pancake

Vegetable Poached Eggs

2 cups chopped broccoli

2 cups chopped spinach (about 3 ounces)

1 cup chopped onion (about 1 large)

1 cup sliced mushrooms (about 3 ounces)

½ cup julienne strips carrot (about 1 medium)

½ cup julienne strips zucchini (about 1 small)

¾ cup marinara sauce

¼ teaspoon pepper

4 eggs

¼ cup shredded part-skim mozzarella cheese (1 ounce)

Spray 12-inch skillet with nonstick cooking spray. Heat skillet over medium heat. Cook broccoli, spinach, onion, mushrooms, carrot and zucchini in skillet 8 to 10 minutes, stirring occasionally, until vegetables are crisp-tender. Stir in marinara sauce and pepper. Cook until thoroughly heated, stirring constantly. Make four 3-inch holes in vegetable mixture, using large spoon. Crack 1 egg into each hole.

Cover and cook about 5 minutes or until egg whites and yolks are firm, not runny. Sprinkle with cheese. Serve immediately. *4 servings*

NUTRITION INFORMATION PER SERVING

ONE SERVING		PERCENT OF U.S. RDA	
Calories	190	Vitamin A	100%
Protein, g	15	Vitamin C	50%
Carbohydrate, g	21	Calcium	22%
Fat, g	8	Iron	20%
Unsaturated	5		
Saturated	3		
Dietary fiber, g	7		
Cholesterol, mg	215		
Sodium, mg	370		

Vegetable Poached Eggs

"Egg-wich"

1½ cups chopped broccoli

½ cup chopped mushrooms

2 tablespoons margarine or butter

1 tablespoon all-purpose flour

¼ teaspoon salt

1 clove garlic, finely chopped

⅔ cup milk

1 egg yolk

4 slices whole wheat bread, toasted

4 eggs

2 teaspoons sesame seed, toasted

Spray 10-inch skillet with nonstick cooking spray. Cook broccoli and mushrooms in skillet about 5 minutes, stirring occasionally, until broccoli is crisp-tender. Heat margarine in 1-quart saucepan over low heat until melted. Stir in flour, salt and garlic. Cook over low heat, stirring constantly, until mixture is smooth and bubbly; remove from heat. Mix milk and egg yolk until smooth; stir into flour mixture. Heat to boiling, stirring constantly. Boil and stir 1 minute. Stir in broccoli mixture.

Cut 2-inch hole in center of each slice toast. Spray same skillet with nonstick cooking spray. Heat skillet over medium heat. Place 1 slice toast in hot skillet; crack 1 egg into hole in toast. Cook until egg white and yolk are firm, not runny. Remove from skillet; keep warm. Repeat with remaining toast and eggs. Top with broccoli mixture. Sprinkle with sesame seed. *4 servings*

NUTRITION INFORMATION PER SERVING

ONE SERVING		PERCENT OF U.S. RDA	
Calories	265	Vitamin A	32%
Protein, g	14	Vitamin C	48%
Carbohydrate, g	23	Calcium	14%
Fat, g	15	Iron	14%
Unsaturated	11		
Saturated	4		
Dietary fiber, g	4		
Cholesterol, mg	270		
Sodium, mg	450		

CHAPTER

5

Satisfying Salads

W e have become familiar with main-dish salads, but we generally think they should have some fish, meat or poultry in them, or it's not a meal. These tempting salads will show you, beyond a shadow of a doubt, that other sources of protein are just as satisfying. Black Bean Taco Salad, Quinoa Primavera Salad, Southwestern Wild Rice Salad and the other delicious salads here will be welcome at any meal. They are also nice for make-ahead meals, to pack for picnics, or to take to work for a hearty lunch.

Ratatouille Salad (*page 108*)

Lentil Salad

2 cups cooled cooked brown or regular long grain rice

1 cup cooled cooked lentils

2 cups bite-size pieces romaine lettuce

1 cup sliced mushrooms (about 3 ounces)

1 cup shredded reduced-fat or regular Cheddar cheese (4 ounces)

1/4 cup chopped fresh cilantro

3 tablespoons lemon juice

1 tablespoon plus 1 teaspoon Dijon mustard

1 tablespoon olive or vegetable oil

1/2 teaspoon Worcestershire sauce

1/8 teaspoon red pepper sauce

2 medium tomatoes, thinly sliced

Mix rice, lentils, lettuce, mushrooms, cheese and cilantro in glass or plastic bowl. Mix remaining ingredients except tomatoes; toss with lentil mixture. Cover and refrigerate at least 30 minutes. Serve on sliced tomatoes. *4 servings*

NUTRITION INFORMATION PER SERVING

ONE SERVING		PERCENT OF U.S. RDA	
Calories	310	Vitamin A	12%
Protein, g	18	Vitamin C	42%
Carbohydrate, g	43	Calcium	24%
Fat, g	10	Iron	20%
Unsaturated	6		
Saturated	4		
Dietary fiber, g	6		
Cholesterol, mg	15		
Sodium, mg	510		

Black Bean Taco Salad

2 cans (15 ounces each) black beans, rinsed and drained

1 can (2 1/4 ounces) sliced ripe olives, drained

1 1/2 cups chopped seeded tomatoes (about 2 medium)

1/3 cup shredded Cheddar cheese

1/4 cup chopped green onions (2 to 3 medium)

1/4 cup chopped fresh cilantro

2 tablespoons lime juice

1 teaspoon ground cumin

1/4 teaspoon pepper

4 cups chopped spinach (about 6 ounces)

Mix beans, olives, tomatoes, cheese, onions and cilantro. Mix lime juice, cumin and pepper; toss with bean mixture. Serve on spinach. *4 servings*

NUTRITION INFORMATION PER SERVING

ONE SERVING		PERCENT OF U.S. RDA	
Calories	325	Vitamin A	56%
Protein, g	23	Vitamin C	62%
Carbohydrate, g	63	Calcium	28%
Fat, g	6	Iron	46%
Unsaturated	3		
Saturated	3		
Dietary fiber, g	18		
Cholesterol, mg	10		
Sodium, mg	740		

Black Bean Taco Salad

Bean Basics

Known as legumes because they come from leguminous plants (ones that produce pods with one row of seeds), beans, peas and lentils are a staple all over the world. Full of soluble fiber, they combine well with grains—especially corn, wheat and rice—for a complete protein.

Adzuki Beans are small, oval, reddish-brown beans with a light, nutty flavor that originated in China and Japan. In Japan, the beans are steamed with rice, imparting a pink blush to the rice, and are served as a festival wedding dish.

Anasazi Beans are maroon-spotted, white, kidney-shaped beans named after the Navajo word meaning "ancient ones." Native Americans still grow these beans in the Southwest. Pinto beans make a nice substitute.

Black Beans, also called turtle beans, are common in the cuisines of South and Central America as well as the Caribbean. They are often served with rice, as the combination makes a complete protein. The popularity of black beans has grown in recent years, and they can be found canned and dried in many supermarkets or in health and ethnic food stores.

Black-eyed Peas, also called black-eyed suzies and cowpeas, are cream-colored with a small, dark brown or black spot on one end. Native to China, black-eyed peas found their way to Africa and then to the southern United States. Black-eyed peas are used in the classic southern dish called hoppin' John.

Butter Beans are cream-colored, large lima beans. They can be found both canned and dried. Often served as a vegetable side dish, they can be added to soups, main dishes and salads.

Cannellini Beans are large white kidney beans. Originally from South America, they have been adopted by Italy and are often mixed with pasta. Look for them with other canned beans.

Fava Beans are large, flat beans that look brown and wrinkly when dried. Sometimes available fresh or canned in ethnic food stores, they have an earthy flavor and are the bean of choice for the Middle Eastern specialty, falafel.

Garbanzo Beans, also called chick-peas, are used in many dishes. Tan, bumpy and round, they have a firm texture and need long, slow cooking. They stand up well to a variety of dishes and are a good addition to soups, stews, casseroles and salads. Garbanzos are used in the popular Middle Eastern dip, hummus. Garbanzo beans are available both canned and dried.

Great Northern Beans are kidney-shaped white beans. They are traditionally used in making baked beans and bean soup, and are commonly available canned and dried.

Kidney Beans are widely available both canned and dried, in shades of dark and light red. They are used to add color and texture to many dishes, and we love them best in chili and red beans and rice.

Lentils are truly an ancient food, known to have been eaten in southwestern Asia around 7,000 B.C. The small grayish-green lentil we are familiar with is only one of the many types and colors of lentils used around the world. They are also available dried in white, yellow, orange, red and black. Lentils are handy because they do not require soaking and cook in a relatively short time.

Lima Beans are available in two sizes—regular and baby. Green limas are good by themselves as a vegetable dish and also make a wonderful addition to multibean salads, soups and casseroles. Limas are occasionally available fresh, but they are most often found frozen or dried. (See also Butter Beans.)

Mung Beans are also known as grams, or when hulled, moong dal. This sweet-flavored bean is native to India and spread to China, where it is extremely popular. Americans know this bean in its sprouted form, either as fresh or canned bean sprouts.

Navy Beans, so called because they fed many a sailor in the early 1800s, are white beans available canned and dried. They are also known as pea beans. Smaller than great northern and cannellini beans, they can be used if navy beans aren't available.

Pinto Beans are two-tone kidney-shaped beans widely used in Central and South American cooking. They turn a uniform pink when cooked, and are used for the Mexican staple, refried beans. They're readily available canned and dried.

Soybeans are not widely eaten in this country as beans. However, we process much of the soybean harvest into oil. Tofu is another product of soybeans with which we have become familiar. This bland, solid bean curd is used in many meatless dishes and combines well with flavorful seasonings.

Split Peas, both green and yellow, are available dried. They do not require soaking and cook relatively quickly. Used mostly in soups, the yellow version is particularly known for pease porridge, referred to in the classic British nursery rhyme.

Kidney

Fava

Lima

Cannellini

Garbanzo

Black

Anasazi

Pinto

Great Northern

Navy

Black-eyed Peas

Mung

Adzuki

Soy

Red Lentil

Lentil

Green Split Pea

Yellow Split Pea

Ratatouille Salad

Ratatouille is a popular dish from the French region of Provence, and it includes eggplant, tomatoes, onions, bell peppers and capers. We've added garbanzo beans to increase the protein.

1 tablespoon olive or vegetable oil

1 small eggplant (about 1 pound), cut into 1-inch cubes

1 cup chopped onion (about 1 large)

1 cup cubed potato (about 1 medium)

2 cloves garlic, finely chopped

1½ cups chopped seeded tomatoes (about 2 medium)

¾ cup chopped green bell pepper (about 1 medium)

3 tablespoons tomato paste

3 tablespoons red wine vinegar

2 tablespoons capers, drained

½ teaspoon Italian seasoning

1 can (15 to 16 ounces) garbanzo beans, rinsed and drained

4 slices wheat bread, toasted and cut into triangles

2 cups spinach leaves (about 3 ounces)

Heat oil in 12-inch nonstick skillet over medium-high heat. Cook eggplant, onion, potato and garlic in oil 8 to 10 minutes, stirring occasionally, until eggplant and potato are crisp-tender. Stir in remaining ingredients except toast and spinach; reduce heat. Cover and simmer 10 minutes. Cover and refrigerate at least 2 hours. Serve over toast and spinach. *4 servings*

NUTRITION INFORMATION PER SERVING

ONE SERVING		PERCENT OF U.S. RDA	
Calories	300	Vitamin A	32%
Protein, g	13	Vitamin C	82%
Carbohydrate, g	56	Calcium	12%
Fat, g	7	Iron	28%
Unsaturated	6		
Saturated	1		
Dietary fiber, g	10		
Cholesterol, mg	0		
Sodium, mg	460		

Kasha Tabbouleh

Serve this salad on a bed of fresh spinach, and add milk, cottage cheese or yogurt to the meal to increase the protein content.

2 cups water

1 package (6¹/₂ ounces) roasted buckwheat kernels (kasha)

1¹/₂ cups finely chopped fresh parsley

1¹/₂ cups chopped seeded tomatoes (about 2 medium)

¹/₃ cup chopped onion (about 1 medium)

¹/₄ cup chopped fresh or 2 teaspoons dried mint leaves

1 small cucumber, peeled and chopped

1 can (15 to 16 ounces) garbanzo beans, rinsed and drained

¹/₄ cup lemon juice

1 tablespoon honey

2 teaspoons Dijon mustard

¹/₄ teaspoon pepper

Lettuce leaves

Heat water to boiling in 2-quart saucepan. Stir in buckwheat kernels. Heat to boiling; reduce heat. Cover and simmer about 25 minutes or until water is absorbed and buckwheat is tender.

Mix buckwheat, parsley, tomatoes, onion, mint, cucumber and beans in glass or plastic bowl. Mix remaining ingredients except salad greens; toss with buckwheat mixture. Cover and refrigerate at least 1 hour. Serve on salad greens. *4 servings*

NUTRITION INFORMATION PER SERVING

ONE SERVING		PERCENT OF U.S. RDA	
Calories	245	Vitamin A	22%
Protein, g	11	Vitamin C	92%
Carbohydrate, g	52	Calcium	10%
Fat, g	3	Iron	28%
Unsaturated	2		
Saturated	1		
Dietary fiber, g	8		
Cholesterol, mg	0		
Sodium, mg	240		

Greek Pasta Salad

4 cups cooked rosamarina (orzo) pasta

2 cups thinly sliced cucumber

³/4 cup chopped tomato (about 1 medium)

¹/2 cup chopped green bell pepper (about 1 small)

¹/2 cup chopped red onion (about ¹/2 medium)

¹/4 cup finely chopped fresh parsley

¹/4 cup olive or vegetable oil

¹/4 cup lemon juice

¹/4 teaspoon salt

1 can (15 to 16 ounces) garbanzo beans, rinsed and drained

1 can (4 ounces) sliced ripe olives,* drained

¹/2 cup crumbled feta cheese

Mix all ingredients except cheese in glass or plastic bowl. Cover and refrigerate at least 1 hour to blend flavors. Top with cheese. *5 servings*

* One-third cup pitted, sliced kalamata or Greek olives can be substituted for the ripe olives.

NUTRITION INFORMATION PER SERVING

ONE SERVING		PERCENT OF U.S. RDA	
Calories	440	Vitamin A	6%
Protein, g	15	Vitamin C	40%
Carbohydrate, g	62	Calcium	14%
Fat, g	18	Iron	28%
Unsaturated	14		
Saturated	4		
Dietary fiber, g	7		
Cholesterol, mg	10		
Sodium, mg	780		

Greek Pasta Salad, Whole Wheat Fettuccine with Spring Vegetables (page 113)

Southwestern Wild Rice Salad

Here's a salad where you can have your bowl, and eat it too! Large, hollowed-out kaiser rolls hold a zesty wild rice and bean filling that just may "bowl" you over!

> 1 cup cooked wild or brown rice
>
> 1 cup cooked brown or regular long grain rice
>
> 3 tablespoons chopped fresh cilantro
>
> 1 can (15 to 16 ounces) pinto beans, rinsed and drained
>
> 1 can (11 ounces) whole kernel corn with red and green peppers, drained
>
> 1 can (4 ounces) chopped green chiles, drained
>
> 3 tablespoons white wine vinegar
>
> 1 tablespoon Dijon mustard
>
> 1/4 teaspoon ground cumin
>
> 1/4 teaspoon pepper
>
> 4 large kaiser rolls
>
> 1/2 cup shredded part-skim mozzarella cheese

Mix wild rice, brown rice, cilantro, beans, corn and chiles. Mix vinegar, mustard, cumin and pepper; toss with rice mixture. Cut 1/2-inch slice from tops of rolls. Remove soft bread from inside of each roll to within 1/2 inch of edge. Reserve bread trimmings for another use. Spoon rice mixture into rolls. Sprinkle with cheese. *4 servings*

NUTRITION INFORMATION PER SERVING

ONE SERVING		PERCENT OF U.S. RDA	
Calories	525	Vitamin A	6%
Protein, g	25	Vitamin C	54%
Carbohydrate, g	107	Calcium	20%
Fat, g	6	Iron	34%
Unsaturated	4		
Saturated	2		
Dietary fiber, g	14		
Cholesterol, mg	10		
Sodium, mg	1610		

Vegetable-Couscous Salad

This bountiful salad is very quick and easy to prepare and tastes wonderful either slightly warm or at room temperature.

> 1 1/2 cups uncooked couscous
>
> 2 cups boiling water
>
> 1/4 teaspoon salt
>
> 1 can (8 ounces) garbanzo beans (rinsed and drained)
>
> 3/4 cup chopped seeded tomato (about 1 medium)
>
> 1/2 cup pesto
>
> 3 tablespoons lemon juice
>
> 1/8 teaspoon pepper
>
> 2 green onions, thinly sliced
>
> 1 can (15 to 16 ounces) kidney beans, rinsed and drained
>
> 4 cups cooked broccoli spears (about 1 pound)

Place couscous in medium bowl. Add boiling water and salt; stir well. Cover and let stand 5 to 7 minutes or until water is absorbed. Stir in remaining ingredients except broccoli. Serve over broccoli. *6 servings*

NUTRITION INFORMATION PER SERVING

ONE SERVING		PERCENT OF U.S. RDA	
Calories	380	Vitamin A	24%
Protein, g	19	Vitamin C	96%
Carbohydrate, g	69	Calcium	16%
Fat, g	9	Iron	26%
Unsaturated	7		
Saturated	2		
Dietary fiber, g	13		
Cholesterol, mg	2		
Sodium, mg	720		

Wheat Berry Salad

Wheat berries are hulled, whole grain wheat kernels. They bring a delightful chewiness to this vibrant, crunchy salad.

> *2¹/₂ cups water*
>
> *1 cup uncooked wheat berries*
>
> *Vinaigrette Dressing (below)*
>
> *1¹/₂ cups broccoli flowerets (about ¹/₂ pound)*
>
> *¹/₂ cup chopped green onions (about 5 medium)*
>
> *¹/₂ cup diced carrot (about 1 medium)*
>
> *1 can (15 to 16 ounces) garbanzo beans, rinsed and drained*

Heat water and wheat berries to boiling in 2-quart saucepan, stirring once or twice; reduce heat. Cover and simmer 50 to 60 minutes or until wheat berries are tender but still crunchy; drain. Prepare Vinaigrette Dressing. Toss wheat berries and remaining ingredients. Cover and refrigerate at least 1 hour. *4 servings*

VINAIGRETTE DRESSING

> *¹/₄ cup balsamic or cider vinegar*
>
> *1 tablespoon chopped fresh or 1 teaspoon dried basil leaves*
>
> *2 tablespoons olive or vegetable oil*
>
> *¹/₄ teaspoon paprika*
>
> *¹/₈ teaspoon salt*
>
> *1 clove garlic, crushed*

Shake all ingredients in tightly covered container.

NUTRITION INFORMATION PER SERVING

ONE SERVING		PERCENT OF U.S. RDA	
Calories	375	Vitamin A	100%
Protein, g	14	Vitamin C	100%
Carbohydrate, g	61	Calcium	10%
Fat, g	9	Iron	22%
Unsaturated	8		
Saturated	1		
Dietary fiber, g	1		
Cholesterol, mg	0		
Sodium, mg	410		

Whole Wheat Fettuccine with Spring Vegetables

> *1 package (12 ounces) whole wheat fettuccine*
>
> *2 cups cut-up asparagus or 1 package (10 ounces) frozen asparagus cuts, thawed*
>
> *2 cups julienne strips zucchini (about 2 medium)*
>
> *1 package (10 ounces) frozen green peas, thawed*
>
> *1 tablespoon margarine or butter*
>
> *³/₄ cup chopped tomato (about 1 medium)*
>
> *¹/₄ cup chopped fresh or 2 tablespoons dried basil leaves*
>
> *¹/₄ teaspoon pepper*
>
> *¹/₂ cup grated Parmesan cheese*

Cook fettuccine as directed on package; drain. Rinse in cold water; drain. Cook asparagus in margarine in 10-inch skillet about 4 minutes, stirring frequently, until crisp-tender. Add zucchini, cook and stir 2 minutes. Mix asparagus mixture, fettuccine, tomato, basil and pepper. Cover and refrigerate about 1 hour or until chilled. Serve with cheese. *6 servings*

NUTRITION INFORMATION PER SERVING

ONE SERVING		PERCENT OF U.S. RDA	
Calories	290	Vitamin A	14%
Protein, g	14	Vitamin C	20%
Carbohydrate, g	48	Calcium	16%
Fat, g	7	Iron	24%
Unsaturated	5		
Saturated	2		
Dietary fiber, g	6		
Cholesterol, mg	55		
Sodium, mg	430		

Quinoa Primavera Salad

Quinoa (pronounced "KEEN-wa") was the staple grain of the Inca Indians in Peru. A small grain with a soft crunch, it can be used in any recipe that calls for rice. Be sure to rinse well before using to remove the bitter-tasting, naturally occurring saponin (nature's insect repellent) that forms on the outside of the kernel.

*10 sun-dried tomatoes (**not oil-packed**)*

1 can (14¹/₂ ounces) ready-to-serve vegetable broth or 1³/₄ cups Vegetable Broth (page 14)

1 cup uncooked quinoa

1 cup frozen green peas

1 can (15 to 16 ounces) pinto beans, rinsed and drained

2 teaspoons vegetable oil

*¹/₂ cup sliced carrot (**about 1 medium**)*

*2 cups sliced zucchini (**about 1 medium**)*

1 small leek, thinly sliced

1 clove garlic, finely chopped

1 tablespoon chopped fresh or 1 teaspoon dried dill weed

3 tablespoons lemon juice

1 tablespoon olive or vegetable oil

Pour enough hot water over sun-dried tomatoes to cover. Let stand 10 to 15 minutes or until softened; drain and cut into halves. Heat broth to boiling in 2-quart saucepan. Stir in quinoa. Heat to boiling; reduce heat to medium. Cover and simmer 10 to 15 minutes or until liquid is absorbed. Mix quinoa, peas, beans and tomatoes in glass or plastic bowl.

Heat 2 teaspoons vegetable oil in 10-inch skillet over medium-high heat. Cook carrot, zucchini, leek and garlic in oil about 8 minutes, stirring frequently, until carrot is crisp-tender. Stir zucchini mixture into quinoa mixture. Mix dill weed, lemon juice and 1 tablespoon olive oil; toss with quinoa mixture. Cover and refrigerate at least 1 hour. *4 servings*

NUTRITION INFORMATION PER SERVING

ONE SERVING		PERCENT OF U.S. RDA	
Calories	365	Vitamin A	100%
Protein, g	16	Vitamin C	26%
Carbohydrate, g	59	Calcium	10%
Fat, g	9	Iron	36%
Unsaturated	8		
Saturated	1		
Dietary fiber, g	4		
Cholesterol, mg	0		
Sodium, mg	360		

Quinoa Primavera Salad

Vegetable Salad Sandwich

Hot salads are popular, and this one showcases salad ingredients that are layered in a hollowed-out bread loaf and then baked.

1 unsliced round loaf whole grain or sourdough bread (8 to 10 inches in diameter)

4 frozen soybean-based vegetable burgers, thawed

1 jar (7¼ ounces) roasted bell peppers, drained and sliced

1 package (16 ounces) frozen cut leaf spinach, thawed and well drained

¼ cup chopped onion (about 1 small)

1 clove garlic, finely chopped

1 medium tomato, thinly sliced

½ cup shredded part-skim or regular mozzarella cheese (2 ounces)

½ teaspoon Italian seasoning

Heat oven to 350°. Cut 1-inch slice from top of bread loaf; set aside. Remove soft bread from inside of loaf to within ¾ inch of edge. Reserve bread trimmings for another use. Arrange burgers on bottom of loaf. Top with bell peppers.

Spray 10-inch skillet with nonstick cooking spray. Cook spinach, onion and garlic in skillet, stirring occasionally, until onion is tender. Spread spinach mixture over bell peppers. Top with tomato. Mix cheese and Italian seasoning; sprinkle evenly over tomato. Replace top of bread. Wrap tightly in aluminum foil. Bake about 40 minutes or until loaf is heated through. Cool 5 minutes. Cut into wedges. *6 servings*

NUTRITION INFORMATION PER SERVING

ONE SERVING		PERCENT OF U.S. RDA	
Calories	335	Vitamin A	70%
Protein, g	20	Vitamin C	64%
Carbohydrate, g	54	Calcium	14%
Fat, g	5	Iron	30%
Unsaturated	3		
Saturated	2		
Dietary fiber, g	2		
Cholesterol, mg	5		
Sodium, mg	330		

Vegetable Salad Sandwich

CHAPTER

6

Pizza, Sandwiches and Breads

The pizzas and sandwiches here are perfect for easy-going dinners, parties, and even snacks. Whip up Italian Polenta Pizza for a teen party or try the Meatless "Meatball" Pizza, made with soybean-based vegetable burgers. Italian Grinders or Mexican Pita Tostadas make quick, tasty dinners, while Mozzarella and Tomato Melts are a snap to whip up at half time or the seventh-inning stretch. You'll also find easy, delicious breads to team with your meals, such as Calico Corn Muffins and Cinnamon-Nut Batter Bread. You'll love the ease and versatility of the pizzas, sandwiches and breads here!

Meatless "Meatball" Pizza (page 122)

Polenta Pizza Casserole

1 cup yellow cornmeal

4 cups milk

½ teaspoon salt

½ cup shredded fresh Parmesan cheese (2 ounces)

½ cup chopped onion (about 1 medium)

¼ cup coarsely chopped green bell pepper

¼ cup coarsely chopped red bell pepper

½ cup sliced mushrooms (about 1½ ounces)

1 clove garlic, finely chopped

2 teaspoons olive or vegetable oil

1½ cups marinara or pizza sauce

1 cup shredded part-skim or regular mozzarella cheese (4 ounces)

¼ cup shredded fresh Parmesan cheese (1 ounce)

1 tablespoon thin strips fresh or 1 teaspoon dried basil leaves

Heat oven to 425°. Grease rectangular baking dish, 13×9×2 inches. Mix cornmeal, milk and salt in 2-quart saucepan. Cook over medium-high heat, stirring constantly, until mixture thickens and boils; reduce heat. Cover and simmer 10 minutes, stirring occasionally; remove from heat. Stir in ½ cup Parmesan cheese. Cool 30 minutes. Spread on bottom and 1 inch up sides of pan.

Cook onion, bell peppers, mushrooms and garlic in oil in 8-inch skillet over medium-high heat, stirring occasionally, until crisp-tender. Spread marinara sauce over cornmeal mixture. Top with cooked vegetables. Sprinkle with cheeses and basil. Bake 18 to 20 minutes or until thoroughly heated and cheese is melted and light golden brown. Let stand 10 minutes. *6 servings*

NUTRITION INFORMATION PER SERVING

ONE SERVING		PERCENT OF U.S. RDA	
Calories	320	Vitamin A	20%
Protein, g	18	Vitamin C	20%
Carbohydrate, g	33	Calcium	50%
Fat, g	14	Iron	10%
Unsaturated	7		
Saturated	7		
Dietary fiber, g	2		
Cholesterol, mg	20		
Sodium, mg	800		

Polenta Pizza Casserole

Meatless "Meatball" Pizza

The "meatballs" here are prepared with 100 percent vegetable burgers flavored with Parmesan cheese and Italian seasoning; they taste just like traditional sausage.

1 Italian bread shell or prepared pizza crust (12 inches in diameter)

2 frozen soybean-based vegetable burgers, thawed

1 tablespoon grated Parmesan cheese

1/2 teaspoon Italian seasoning, crumbled

3/4 cup pizza sauce

2 tablespoons sliced ripe olives

1 cup shredded part-skim or regular mozzarella cheese (4 ounces)

1 cup shredded provolone cheese (4 ounces)

Heat oven to 425°. Place bread shell on ungreased large cookie sheet. Spread pizza sauce over bread shell. Mix burgers, Parmesan cheese and Italian seasoning. Shape into 1/2-inch balls. Top with burger balls and olives. Sprinkle with cheeses. Bake 18 to 20 minutes or until cheese is melted and light golden brown. *6 servings*

NUTRITION INFORMATION PER SERVING

ONE SERVING		PERCENT OF U.S. RDA	
Calories	203	Vitamin A	6%
Protein, g	16	Vitamin C	*
Carbohydrate, g	10	Calcium	30%
Fat, g	11	Iron	8%
Unsaturated	5		
Saturated	6		
Dietary fiber, g	0		
Cholesterol, mg	25		
Sodium, mg	490		

Mediterranean Pizza

1 Italian bread shell or prepared pizza crust (12 inches in diameter)

1 can (15 to 16 ounces) garbanzo beans, drained and 1/4 cup liquid reserved

1 tablespoon chopped fresh or 1 teaspoon dried oregano leaves

1 small red onion, thinly sliced and separated into rings (about 1/2 cup)

1 can (14 ounces) artichoke hearts, drained and cut into fourths

1/3 cup kalamata or ripe olives, pitted and cut into fourths

1/3 cup chopped yellow or orange bell pepper

2 tablespoons chopped sun-dried tomatoes in oil, drained

1 1/2 cups shredded part-skim or regular mozzarella cheese (6 ounces)

1/2 cup feta cheese, crumbled

Heat oven to 425°. Place bread shell on ungreased large cookie sheet. Place beans and 1/4 cup bean liquid in blender or food processor. Cover and blend or process until smooth. Mix bean mixture and oregano; spread over bread shell. Top with onion rings, artichoke hearts, olives, bell pepper and tomatoes. Sprinkle with cheeses. Bake 15 to 20 minutes or until cheese is melted and light golden brown. *6 servings*

NUTRITION INFORMATION PER SERVING

ONE SERVING		PERCENT OF U.S. RDA	
Calories	430	Vitamin A	10%
Protein, g	20	Vitamin C	14%
Carbohydrate, g	57	Calcium	32%
Fat, g	16	Iron	26%
Unsaturated	8		
Saturated	8		
Dietary fiber, g	6		
Cholesterol, mg	25		
Sodium, mg	1060		

Four-Cheese Pesto Pizza

6 whole wheat or white pita breads (6 inches in diameter)

1 package (8 ounces) light cream cheese (Neufchâtel) or regular cream cheese, softened

2 tablespoons milk

6 tablespoons pesto

1 can (2¼ ounces) sliced ripe olives, drained

½ cup shredded part-skim or regular mozzarella cheese (3 ounces)

½ cup shredded Fontina or provolone cheese (3 ounces)

2 tablespoons grated Parmesan cheese

2 tablespoons chopped fresh parsley

Heat oven to 425°. Place pita breads on ungreased large cookie sheet. Mix cream cheese and milk until smooth. Spread on pita breads to within ¼ inch of edge. Gently spread pesto over cream cheese. Top with olives. Sprinkle with cheeses and parsley. Bake 7 to 12 minutes or until thoroughly heated and cheese is melted. *6 servings*

NUTRITION INFORMATION PER SERVING

ONE SERVING		PERCENT OF U.S. RDA	
Calories	455	Vitamin A	14%
Protein, g	22	Vitamin C	2%
Carbohydrate, g	49	Calcium	40%
Fat, g	22	Iron	16%
Unsaturated	11		
Saturated	11		
Dietary fiber, g	7		
Cholesterol, mg	45		
Sodium, mg	1070		

Pita Pizzas

4 whole wheat pita breads (6 inches in diameter)

¼ cup chopped onion (about 1 small)

1 small clove garlic, finely chopped

1 can (15 to 16 ounces) great northern beans, drained and ¼ cup liquid reserved

2 tablespoons chopped fresh or 2 teaspoons dried basil leaves

1 large tomato, seeded and cut into ¼-inch pieces

1 large green bell pepper, cut into 16 thin rings

1 cup shredded part-skim or regular mozzarella cheese (4 ounces)

Heat oven to 425°. Cut pita breads around edge in half, using knife. Place in ungreased jelly roll pan, 15½×10½×1 inch. Bake uncovered about 5 minutes or just until crisp. Cook onion and garlic in reserved bean liquid in 10-inch nonstick skillet over medium heat 5 minutes, stirring occasionally. Stir in beans; heat through.

Place bean mixture and basil in blender or food processor. Cover and blend or process until smooth. Spread about 2 tablespoons bean mixture on each pita bread half. Top with tomato and bell pepper. Sprinkle with cheese. Bake in jelly roll pan 5 to 7 minutes or until cheese is melted. *4 servings*

NUTRITION INFORMATION PER SERVING

ONE SERVING		PERCENT OF U.S. RDA	
Calories	305	Vitamin A	10%
Protein, g	22	Vitamin C	28%
Carbohydrate, g	50	Calcium	38%
Fat, g	6	Iron	34%
Unsaturated	2		
Saturated	4		
Dietary fiber, g	9		
Cholesterol, mg	15		
Sodium, mg	580		

Cajun Muffulettas

The muffuletta is a classic New Orleans sand-wich, typically made with salami and ham. In our version, pureed black-eyed peas, also a Southern favorite, replace the meat.

Olive Salad (below)

1 can (15 to 16 ounces) black-eyed peas, rinsed and drained

¼ cup water

1 teaspoon red pepper sauce

4 large kaiser rolls

4 slices provolone cheese

4 slices tomato

Prepare Olive Salad. Place peas, water and pepper sauce in blender or food processor. Cover and blend or process until smooth. Cut ½-inch slice from tops of rolls; set aside. Remove soft bread from inside of each roll to within ½ inch of edge. Reserve bread trimmings for another use. Spread about ¼ cup pea mixture in each roll. Top each with cheese slice, tomato slice and scant 2 table-spoons Olive Salad. Cover with tops of rolls. *4 sandwiches*

OLIVE SALAD

¼ cup chopped pimiento-stuffed olives

¼ cup chopped kalamata or ripe olives

¼ cup sliced hot pickled okra (from 16-ounce jar)

1 tablespoon chopped fresh parsley

1 tablespoon olive or vegetable oil

¼ teaspoon dried oregano leaves, crumbled

⅛ teaspoon pepper

1 small clove garlic, finely chopped

Mix all ingredients. Cover and refrigerate at least 1 hour to blend flavors.

NUTRITION INFORMATION PER SERVING

ONE SANDWICH		PERCENT OF U.S. RDA	
Calories	450	Vitamin A	10%
Protein, g	23	Vitamin C	6%
Carbohydrate, g	69	Calcium	28%
Fat, g	16	Iron	32%
Unsaturated	9		
Saturated	7		
Dietary fiber, g	15		
Cholesterol, mg	25		
Sodium, mg	1310		

Fruited Gorgonzola and Cheddar Melts

For a change of pace, try serving this delecta-ble sandwich for breakfast or brunch.

4 slices bread, each 1 inch thick

1 large apple, cored and cut into 8 rings

1 large ripe pear, sliced

4 ounces Cheddar cheese, sliced

4 ounces Gorgonzola cheese, crumbled

Set oven control to broil. Place bread on un-greased cookie sheet. Broil with tops about 4 inches from heat until golden brown; turn. Divide apple rings and pear slices among bread slices. Top with cheeses. Broil just until cheese begins to melt. *4 sandwiches*

NUTRITION INFORMATION PER SERVING

ONE SANDWICH		PERCENT OF U.S. RDA	
Calories	355	Vitamin A	12%
Protein, g	16	Vitamin C	4%
Carbohydrate, g	34	Calcium	32%
Fat, g	19	Iron	7%
Unsaturated	7		
Saturated	12		
Dietary fiber, g	4		
Cholesterol, mg	50		
Sodium, mg	720		

Fruited Gorgonzola and Cheddar Melts

Italian Grinders

4 frozen soybean-based vegetable burgers, thawed

3 tablespoons grated Parmesan cheese

1 teaspoon Italian seasoning

4 teaspoons olive or vegetable oil

1 small onion, sliced

1 small red bell pepper, cut into 1/4-inch strips

1 small green bell pepper, cut into 1/4-inch strips

4 frankfurter buns, split

1/2 cup spaghetti sauce, heated

Mix burgers, cheese and Italian seasoning. Shape into 16 balls. Heat 2 teaspoons of the oil in 10-inch nonstick skillet over medium heat until hot. Cook burger balls in oil, turning frequently, until brown. Remove from skillet; keep warm.

Heat remaining 2 teaspoons oil in same skillet over medium heat until hot. Cook onion and bell peppers in oil, stirring frequently, until crisp-tender. Place 4 burger balls in each bun. Top with vegetable mixture. Serve with spaghetti sauce. *4 servings*

NUTRITION INFORMATION PER SERVING

ONE SERVING		PERCENT OF U.S. RDA	
Calories	335	Vitamin A	8%
Protein, g	22	Vitamin C	68%
Carbohydrate, g	35	Calcium	22%
Fat, g	13	Iron	32%
Unsaturated	10		
Saturated	3		
Dietary fiber, g	2		
Cholesterol, mg	5		
Sodium, mg	640		

Italian Grinders, Cajun Muffulettas (page 124)

Mexican Pita Tostadas

1 can (15 ounces) black beans, drained and 3 tablespoons liquid reserved

1 1/2 teaspoons ground cumin

1 1/2 teaspoons chile powder

1/8 teaspoon ground red pepper (cayenne)

4 white or whole wheat pita breads (6 inches in diameter)

1/4 cup chopped red bell pepper

1/4 cup chopped green bell pepper

2 tablespoons chopped green onions

1/2 cup shredded Cheddar cheese (2 ounces)

1/2 cup shredded Monterey Jack cheese (2 ounces)

1/2 cup shredded lettuce

1/4 cup chopped fresh cilantro

1/2 cup salsa

Sour cream, if desired

Place beans, reserved bean liquid, cumin, chile powder and red pepper in blender or food processor. Cover and blend or process until smooth. Spread bean mixture on pita breads. Top with bell peppers, onions, cheeses, lettuce and cilantro. Serve with salsa. Garnish with sour cream. *4 servings*

NUTRITION INFORMATION PER SERVING

ONE SERVING		PERCENT OF U.S. RDA	
Calories	465	Vitamin A	16%
Protein, g	24	Vitamin C	20%
Carbohydrate, g	77	Calcium	32%
Fat, g	11	Iron	30%
Unsaturated	5		
Saturated	6		
Dietary fiber, g	10		
Cholesterol, mg	30		
Sodium, mg	850		

What Is Textured Vegetable Protein?

Textured vegetable protein is a basic soybean product that is used to replace animal-source protein and is available in many forms. After processing, it is packaged in either plain or seasoned dehydrated form to which water is added, or in ready-to-use plain or seasoned frozen products.

Soybean History

Generally accepted as the highest quality of vegetable protein, the soybean is also one of the most plentiful with crops yielding 60 million metric tons per year. The first written record of soybeans is dated 2838 B.C. and they have been cultivated for human food in China for thousands of years. So important are soybeans in Chinese culture, that they are considered one of the five sacred grains, along with rice, wheat, barley and millet, even though they are a legume. The versatile soybean found its way from China to Japan to Europe and then to the United States in the 1920's. One-third of the world's soybean crop is now produced in the United States.

Product Versatility

Today's soybean derived foods are better and more numerous than ever before. The versatile array of products can be used to replace ground meat and the naturally bland flavor of soy allows for creating a wide variety of flavors. Textured vegetable protein has a chewy texture very similar to ground meat but because it has a low moisture and fat content, it has the added advantage of not shrinking during cooking. This product also has a very short cooking time.

Recipe Use in This Book

The recipes we've developed for this book utilize the frozen soybean-based vegetable burgers. We've chosen these because in our testing, we discovered that vegetable burgers made without a legume or soybean base and containing only vegetables, such as carrots, zucchini and mushrooms, tend to fall apart more easily when cooked in another mixture.

Nutrition

The excellent nutritive value of soybeans was not scientifically confirmed until the 20th century. Unlike other legumes, soybeans are high in digestible protein and low in carbohydrate. As with all legumes, soybeans do not contain cholesterol, are low in saturated fat, and contain dietary fiber. Soybeans are extremely versatile and are used to produce food products such as: tofu, soybean oil, soy flour, soy milk, soy sauce and bean sprouts. Other products made from soybean by-products include: margarine, food emulsifiers, animal feed, soap and plastics.

Mozzarella and Tomato Melts

4 slices Italian bread, each 1 inch thick

8 ounces part-skim mozzarella cheese, sliced

2 medium tomatoes, thinly sliced

Salt and freshly ground pepper to taste

½ cup pesto

Set oven control to broil. Place bread on rack in broiler pan. Broil with tops about 4 inches from heat until golden brown; turn. Divide cheese among bread slices. Broil just until cheese begins to melt. Arrange tomatoes on cheese. Sprinkle with salt and pepper. Top with pesto. Garnish with fresh basil leaves if desired. *4 open-face sandwiches*

NUTRITION INFORMATION PER SERVING

ONE SANDWICH		PERCENT OF U.S. RDA	
Calories	355	Vitamin A	12%
Protein, g	20	Vitamin C	10%
Carbohydrate, g	23	Calcium	50%
Fat, g	21	Iron	10%
Unsaturated	13		
Saturated	8		
Dietary fiber, g	2		
Cholesterol, mg	35		
Sodium, mg	940		

Grilled Peanut Butter and Banana

8 slices English muffin bread

½ cup peanut butter

2 medium bananas

Margarine or butter, softened

Spread 4 slices bread with peanut butter. Slice bananas and arrange on peanut butter. Top with remaining slices bread; spread top slices bread with margarine. Place sandwiches, margarine sides down, in skillet. Spread top slices bread with margarine. Cook uncovered over medium heat about 4 minutes or until bottoms are golden brown; turn. Cook 2 to 3 minutes longer or until bottoms are golden brown and peanut butter is melted. *4 sandwiches*

NUTRITION INFORMATION PER SERVING

ONE SANDWICH		PERCENT OF U.S. RDA	
Calories	470	Vitamin A	10%
Protein, g	13	Vitamin C	4%
Carbohydrate, g	69	Calcium	20%
Fat, g	18	Iron	20%
Unsaturated	14		
Saturated	4		
Dietary fiber, g	5		
Cholesterol, mg	0		
Sodium, mg	750		

Bean Patties

Guacamole Sauce (right)

1 can (16 ounces) vegetarian refried beans

1 can (4 ounces) chopped green chiles, drained

1 egg, slightly beaten

½ cup dry bread crumbs

¼ cup chopped onion (about 1 small)

¼ cup shredded Cheddar cheese (1 ounce)

½ teaspoon salt

2 tablespoons vegetable oil

Prepare Guacamole Sauce. Mix beans, chiles, egg, bread crumbs, onion, cheese and salt. Heat oil in nonstick 10-inch skillet. Drop bean mixture by 4 spoonfuls into skillet; flatten and shape into patties, each 1 inch thick. Cook over medium heat about 5 minutes on each side or until hot and brown. Top with Guacamole Sauce. *4 servings*

GUACAMOLE SAUCE

¾ cup finely chopped seeded tomato (about 1 medium)

2 tablespoons finely chopped onion

1 tablespoon finely chopped cilantro leaves, if desired

1 tablespoon lemon juice

¼ teaspoon salt

4 drops red pepper sauce

1 small ripe avocado, mashed

1 clove garlic, crushed

Mix all ingredients. Cover and refrigerate at least 1 hour.

NUTRITION INFORMATION PER SERVING

ONE SERVING		PERCENT OF U.S. RDA	
Calories	345	Vitamin A	10%
Protein, g	13	Vitamin C	30%
Carbohydrate, g	39	Calcium	12%
Fat, g	19	Iron	20%
Unsaturated	14		
Saturated	5		
Dietary fiber, g	9		
Cholesterol, mg	60		
Sodium, mg	1370		

Savory Rosemary Scones

These wonderful, hearty scones have just a touch of sweetness. They are an especially nice addition to an Italian main dish.

1½ cups all-purpose flour

½ cup whole wheat flour

½ cup rye flour

2 tablespoons packed dark brown sugar

1½ teaspoons baking powder

½ teaspoon baking soda

1 cup vanilla nonfat or regular yogurt

¼ cup grated Parmesan cheese

¼ cup chopped red bell pepper

⅓ cup Egg Substitute (page 88) or cholesterol-free egg product or 1 egg plus 1 egg white

2 tablespoons margarine or butter, softened

½ teaspoon dried rosemary leaves, crumbled

2 teaspoons water

1 tablespoon grated Parmesan cheese

Heat oven to 375°. Grease cookie sheet. Mix flours, brown sugar, baking powder and baking soda in large bowl. Mix yogurt, ¼ cup Parmesan cheese, the bell pepper, Egg Substitute, margarine and rosemary. Stir yogurt mixture into flour mixture just until moistened.

Turn dough onto lightly floured surface; gently roll in flour to coat. Knead lightly 10 times. Pat or roll ½ inch thick on cookie sheet. Cut into 12 wedges, but do not separate. Brush with water. Sprinkle with 1 tablespoon Parmesan cheese. Bake 20 to 25 minutes or until golden brown. Cool 5 minutes. Separate into wedges. *12 scones*

NUTRITION INFORMATION PER SERVING

ONE SCONE		PERCENT OF U.S. RDA	
Calories	140	Vitamin A	12%
Protein, g	5	Vitamin C	*
Carbohydrate, g	25	Calcium	10%
Fat, g	3	Iron	8%
Unsaturated	2		
Saturated	1		
Dietary fiber, g	2		
Cholesterol, mg	2		
Sodium, mg	170		

Savory Walnut Hearth Bread

1 cup all-purpose flour

1 cup whole wheat flour

$^1/_2$ cup rye flour

$^1/_2$ cup bran cereal shreds

2 teaspoons baking powder

1 teaspoon salt

1 teaspoon regular or quick-acting active
  dry yeast

$^1/_2$ cup chopped green onions (about 5
  medium)

$^1/_4$ cup chopped walnuts

1$^1/_4$ cups buttermilk

3 tablespoons packed brown sugar

2 tablespoons vegetable oil

2 eggs

Heat oven to 350°. Grease 3-quart casserole. Mix flours, cereal, baking powder, salt and yeast in large bowl. Mix remaining ingredients; stir into flour mixture just until moistened. Turn dough into casserole. Bake about 45 minutes or until golden brown and toothpick inserted in center comes out clean. Remove from casserole. Cool on wire rack. *1 loaf (16 slices)*

NUTRITION INFORMATION PER SERVING

ONE SLICE		PERCENT OF U.S. RDA	
Calories	125	Vitamin A	4%
Protein, g	4	Vitamin C	*
Carbohydrate, g	20	Calcium	6%
Fat, g	4	Iron	6%
Unsaturated	3		
Saturated	1		
Dietary fiber, g	2		
Cholesterol, mg	25		
Sodium, mg	220		

Calico Corn Muffins

$^1/_2$ cup yellow cornmeal

$^1/_2$ cup all-purpose flour

$^1/_2$ cup milk

1 tablespoon sugar

2 tablespoons vegetable oil

2 teaspoons baking powder

$^1/_4$ teaspoon salt

1 egg

$^1/_2$ cup frozen corn with red and green
  peppers, thawed

Heat oven to 425°. Grease bottoms only of 8 medium muffin cups, 2$^1/_2$×1$^1/_4$ inches. Mix all ingredients except corn about 20 seconds or until dry ingredients are moistened. Beat vigorously 1 minute. Stir in corn. Fill muffin cups two-thirds full. Bake about 15 minutes or until golden brown. Immediately remove from pan. *8 muffins*

NUTRITION INFORMATION PER SERVING

ONE SLICE		PERCENT OF U.S. RDA	
Calories	120	Vitamin A	2%
Protein, g	3	Vitamin C	*
Carbohydrate, g	17	Calcium	8%
Fat, g	5	Iron	4%
Unsaturated	4		
Saturated	1		
Dietary fiber, g	1		
Cholesterol, mg	30		
Sodium, mg	200		

Cinnamon-Nut Batter Bread

1 package regular or quick-acting active dry yeast

1¹/₂ cups warm water (105° to 115°)

1 teaspoon vanilla

2 cups all-purpose flour

2 tablespoons honey

2 tablespoons margarine or butter, softened

¹/₂ teaspoon salt

1 cup whole wheat flour

¹/₂ cup quick-cooking or regular oats

¹/₂ cup chopped pecans or walnuts

1 teaspoon ground cinnamon

Dissolve yeast in warm water and vanilla in large bowl. Add all-purpose flour, honey, margarine and salt. Beat on medium speed 2 minutes, scraping bowl occasionally. Stir in remaining ingredients until well blended. Scrape batter from side of bowl. Cover and let rise in warm place 45 to 60 minutes or until almost double.

Spray 1¹/₂-quart casserole with nonstick cooking spray. Stir down batter by beating about 25 strokes. Spread batter in casserole; smooth and pat batter, using floured hand. Cover and let rise in warm place about 30 minutes or until double. (Batter is ready if indentation remains when touched.)

Heat oven to 350°. Bake 35 to 40 minutes or until loaf sounds hollow when tapped. Immediately remove from casserole. Cool on wire rack. *1 loaf (12 slices)*

NUTRITION INFORMATION PER SERVING

ONE SLICE		PERCENT OF U.S. RDA	
Calories	190	Vitamin A	6%
Protein, g	4	Vitamin C	2%
Carbohydrate, g	30	Calcium	*
Fat, g	6	Iron	10%
Unsaturated	5		
Saturated	1		
Dietary fiber, g	3		
Cholesterol, mg	0		
Sodium, mg	110		

Easy Brown Bread

1 cup all-purpose or rye flour

1 cup whole wheat flour

1 cup yellow cornmeal

1 cup dried cherries, cranberries or raisins

2 cups buttermilk

³/₄ cup molasses

2 teaspoons baking soda

2 teaspoons vanilla

¹/₂ teaspoon salt

Heat oven to 325°. Grease 2-quart casserole. Beat all ingredients in large bowl on low speed 30 seconds, scraping bowl constantly. Beat on medium speed 30 seconds, scraping bowl constantly. Pour into casserole. Bake about 1 hour or until loaf sounds hollow when tapped; remove from casserole. Cool on wire rack. *1 loaf (12 slices)*

NUTRITION INFORMATION PER SERVING

ONE SLICE		PERCENT OF U.S. RDA	
Calories	220	Vitamin A	*
Protein, g	5	Vitamin C	*
Carbohydrate, g	50	Calcium	10%
Fat, g	1	Iron	14%
Unsaturated	0		
Saturated	1		
Dietary fiber, g	2		
Cholesterol, mg	2		
Sodium, mg	280		

METRIC CONVERSION GUIDE

U.S. UNITS	CANADIAN METRIC	AUSTRALIAN METRIC
Volume		
1/4 teaspoon	1 mL	1 ml
1/2 teaspoon	2 mL	2 ml
1 teaspoon	5 mL	5 ml
1 tablespoon	15 mL	20 ml
1/4 cup	50 mL	60 ml
1/3 cup	75 mL	80 ml
1/2 cup	125 mL	125 ml
2/3 cup	150 mL	170 ml
3/4 cup	175 mL	190 ml
1 cup	250 mL	250 ml
1 quart	1 liter	1 liter
1 1/2 quarts	1.5 liter	1.5 liter
2 quarts	2 liters	2 liters
2 1/2 quarts	2.5 liters	2.5 liters
3 quarts	3 liters	3 liters
4 quarts	4 liters	4 liters
Weight		
1 ounce	30 grams	30 grams
2 ounces	55 grams	60 grams
3 ounces	85 grams	90 grams
4 ounces (1/4 pound)	115 grams	125 grams
8 ounces (1/2 pound)	225 grams	225 grams
16 ounces (1 pound)	455 grams	500 grams
1 pound	455 grams	1/2 kilogram

Measurements		**Temperatures**	
Inches	Centimeters	Fahrenheit	Celsius
1	2.5	32°	0°
2	5.0	212°	100°
3	7.5	250°	120°
4	10.0	275°	140°
5	12.5	300°	150°
6	15.0	325°	160°
7	17.5	350°	180°
8	20.5	375°	190°
9	23.0	400°	200°
10	25.5	425°	220°
11	28.0	450°	230°
12	30.5	475°	240°
13	33.0	500°	260°
14	35.5		
15	38.0		

NOTE
The recipes in this cookbook have not been developed or tested using metric measures. When converting recipes to metric, some variations in quality may be noted.

134

Index

(Page numbers in *italics* indicate
  photographs.)

A
Anasazi Enchiladas, *31*, 34
Angel Hair Patties, 79
Asian Omelet, 96–97

B
Baked Chile in Polenta Crust, 26
Baked Lentils with Tarragon Rice, 38
Baked Orzo and Vegetables, 45
Baked Polenta Supper, 40
Baked Risotto, 44
Barley-Vegetable Sauté, 77
Basil Crème Fraîche, 16
Bean and Pepper Chile, 25
Bean Basics, 106–107
Bean Patties, 130
Black Bean(s)
  Enchiladas, 61
  and Rice, 33
  Soup, Southwestern, 8
  Stew, Spicy, 20
  Taco Salad, *102*, 104
  -Tortilla Pie, 32
Bread
  Brown, Easy, 133
  Cajun Muffulettas, 124, *126*

Calico Corn Muffins, 132
Cinnamon-Nut Batter, *92*, 133
Savory Rosemary Scones, 131
Savory Walnut Hearth, 132
Spoon, Spicy Five-Pepper, *56*, 57
Broccoli and Swiss Cheese Frittata,
  90–91

C
Cabbage, Stuffed, 62–63
Cabbage-Bean Soup with Rivels, 9
Cajun Muffulettas, 124, *126*
Calico Corn Muffins, 132
Caribbean Black Beans, 62
Caribbean Stew with Pineapple Salsa,
  22
Casseroles, 31–57
  Anasazi Enchiladas, *31*, 34
  Baked Lentils with Tarragon Rice,
    38
  Baked Orzo and Vegetables, 45
  Baked Polenta Supper, 40
  Baked Risotto, 44
  Black Beans and Rice, 33
  Black Bean-Tortilla Pie, 32
  Fall Vegetable Bake, 53
  Indian Mixed Beans and Rice, 37
  Kasha and Cabbage, 45
  Lentil Loaf, 38, *39*

Macaroni and Cheese, 46
Minted Couscous and Red Lentil
  Pilaf, 46
Mixed Pepper and Bean Chile, 36
Moussaka, 42
Mushroom and Spinach Lasagne, 51
Pasta e Fagioli Stew, 48
Pasta Torte, 48, *49*
Phyllo and Spinach Pie, 53
Pizza Pot Pie, *43*, 44
Polenta Pizza, 120, *121*
Polenta with Cheese, 40
Quinoa-Vegetable Bake, 41
Savory Bread Pudding, 55
Savory Southwest Loaf, 41
Southern Peas and Greens, 34–35
Southwest Vegetable Stew with Corn
  Bread Topping, 36–37
Spicy Five-Pepper Spoon Bread, *56*,
  57
Spinach-Fennel Kugel, 52
Tabbouleh, 42
Three-Cheese Noodle Bake, 52
Vegetable Manicotti, 47
Vegetable Shepherd's Pie, 54
Winter Baked Pasta, *50*, 51
Winter Root Vegetable, 55
Zucchini-Pesto, 35
Cheesy tomato filling, 95

Chile
    Baked, in Polenta Crust, 26
    Bean and Pepper, 25
    Chunky Vegetable, 25
    Cincinnati, 27
    Tex-Mex, 24
    Three-Bean, 24
    Three-Bean White, 29
Chunky Vegetable Chile, 25
Cilantro Cream, 18
Cincinnati Chile, 27
Cinnamon-Nut Batter Bread, *92*, 133
Corn bread topping, 37
Corn Chowder, Santa Fe, 2
Corn Muffins, Calico, 132
Crème Fraîche, Basil, 16
Creole sauce, 91
Crunchy Bean Skillet, 60
Curried Lentils and Barley, 72
Curried Stew with Peanut Sauce, 20–21
Curried Yellow Split Pea Soup with Cilantro Cream, 18

D
Dill Dumplings, 21
Double Spinach Fettucine, 79
Dressing, Vinaigrette, 113
Dumplings, Dill, 21

E
Easy Baked Stew, 19
Easy Brown Bread, 133
Easy Oven Pancake, 98, *99*
Egg Burrito Grande, 97
Egg dishes. *See* Frittatas, *and* Quiches, Omelets, and other egg dishes
Eggplant Parmigiana, Layered, 84
Egg Substitute, 88
"Egg-wich," 101

F
Fall Vegetable Bake, 53
Filling, Cheesy Tomato, 95
Four-Cheese Pesto Pizza, 123
Frittatas
    Broccoli and Swiss Cheese, 90–91
    Southwestern, *92*, 93
    Spinach, with Creole Sauce, 91
Fruited Gorgonzola and Cheddar Melts, 124, *125*

G
Garden Phyllo Quiches, *87*, 90
Garden Vegetable Stew, 23
Gazpacho with Basil Crème Fraîche, 16, *17*
Glossary, x–xiii
Grains
    Cooking Chart, 66–67
    types of, 64–65
Greek Pasta Salad, 110, *111*
Green Jerked Chile, 28
Grilled Peanut Butter and Banana, 129
Guacamole Sauce, 130

I
Indian Mixed Beans and Rice, 37
Indian Split Peas with Vegetables, 73
Italian Grinders, *126*, 127

K
Kasha and Cabbage, 45
Kasha Tabbouleh, 109

L
Layered Eggplant Parmigiana, 84
Legumes
    Cooking chart, 11–13
    selection, storage and cooking tips, 10
    soaking, 10
Lentils
    Curried, and Barley, 72
    Loaf, 38, *39*
    Minted Couscous and Red Lentil Pilaf, 46
    Ratatouille, 73
    Risotto, Squash-and-, 72
    Salad, 104
    -Spinach Soup, 18
    and Vegetables, Southern, 3, *6*
    and Vegetable Stew, 19

M
Macaroni and Cheese, 46
Meatless cuisine, vii–viii
    planning, ix
Meatless "Meatball" Pizza, *118*, 122
Mediterranean Pizza, 122
Mediterranean Vegetable Soup, 14
Menus, xiv–xv
    planning, xvi–xix
    30-minute, 94

Mexican Pita Tostadas, 127
Mexican Strata, 96
Minted Couscous and Red Lentil Pilaf, 46
Mixed Pepper and Bean Chile, 36
Moroccan Garbanzo Beans with Raisins, 60
Moussaka, 42
Mozzarella and Tomato Melts, 129
Mushroom and Spinach Lasagne, 51
Mushroom Paprikàs, 76

N
Noodles Romanoff, 78

O
Olive Salad, 124

P
Paella, Spring Vegetable, *68*, 69
Pasta e Fagioli Stew, 48
Pasta Salad, Greek, 110, *111*
Pasta Torte, 48, *49*
Peanut Butter and Banana, Grilled, 129
Peanut Sauce, 21
Phyllo and Spinach Pie, 53
Pineapple Salsa, 22
Pita Pizzas, 123
Pizza, 119–133
    Four-Cheese Pesto, 123
    Meatless "Meatball," *118*, 122
    Mediterranean, 122
    Pita, 123
Pizza Pot Pie, *43*, 44
Pizza Soup, *4*, 5
Polenta
    with Cheese, 40
    Crust, 26
    Crust, Baked Chile in, 26
    with Italian Vegetables, 74, *75*
    Pizza Casserole, 120, *121*
    Supper, Baked, 40
Protein, vii
    complementing combinations, viii–x
    textured vegetable, 128

Q
Quiches, Omelets, and other egg dishes. *See also* Frittatas
    Asian Omelet, 96–97
    Blue Cheese Omelet with Pears, 93

Easy Oven Pancake, 98, *99*
Egg Burrito Grande, 97
Egg Substitute, 88
"Egg-wich," 101
Garden Phyllo Quiches, *86*, 90
Mexican Strata, 96
Rice and Bean Quiche, 88, *89*
Rolled Cheese Souffle, 95
Tex-Mex Scrambled Eggs, 98
Vegetable Poached Eggs, *100*, 101
Quinoa
  and Bulgur Pilaf, 77
  Primavera Salad, *114*, 115
  Vegetable Bake, 41

R
Ratatouille
  Lentil, 73
  Salad, *105*, 108
Rice
  and Bean Quiche, 88, *89*
  Black Beans and, 33
  Cooking Chart, 66–67
  Tarragon, Baked Lentils with, 38
Risotto
  Baked, 44
  Florentine, 76
  Squash-and-Lentil, 72
Rivels, 9
Roasted Vegetable Broth, 15
Rolled Cheese Souffle, 95
Root Vegetables with Citrus Sauce, 85

S
Salads, 103–117
  Black Bean Taco, *102*, 104
  Greek Pasta, 110, *111*
  Kasha Tabbouleh, 109
  Lentil, 104
  Olive, 124
  Quinoa Primavera, *114*, 115
  Ratatouille, *105*, 108
  Southwestern Wild Rice, 112
  Vegetable-Couscous, 112
  Vegetable Salad Sandwich, *116*, 117
  Wheat Berry, 113
  Whole Wheat Fettucine with Spring
    Vegetables, 111, *113*
Salsa
  Pineapple, 22
  Tomatillo, 29
  Tomato, 70

Sandwiches
  Bean Patties, 130
  Fruited Gorgonzola and Cheddar
    Melts, 124, *125*
  Italian Grinders, *126*, 127
  Mexican Pita Tostadas, 127
  Mozzarella and Tomato Melts, 129
Santa Fe Corn Chowder, 2
Sauce(s)
  Cilantro Cream, 18
  Creole, 91
  Guacamole, 130
  Peanut, 21
Sautéed Bean Cake with Tomato Salsa,
  70, *71*
Savory Bread Pudding, 55
Savory Rosemary Scones, 131
Savory Southwest Loaf, 41
Savory Walnut Hearth Bread, 132
Sicilian Fusilli, *80*, 81
Skillet dishes, 59–85
  Angel Hair Patties, 79
  Black Bean Enchiladas, 61
  Caribbean Black Beans, 62
  Crunchy Bean Skillet, 60
  Curried Lentils and Barley, 72
  Double Spinach Fettucine, 79
  Indian Split Peas with Vegetables,
    73
  Layered Eggplant Parmigiana, 84
  Lentil Ratatouille, 73
  Moroccan Garbanzo Beans with
    Raisins, 60
  Mushroom Paprikas, 76
  Noodles Romanoff, 78
  Polenta with Italian Vegetables, 74,
    75
  Quinoa and Bulgur Pilaf, 77
  Risotto Florentine, 76
  Root Vegetables with Citrus Sauce,
    85
  Sicilian Fusilli, *80*, 81
  Spaghetti and Spicy Rice Balls, 81
  Spicy Bulgur-and-Barley Balls, 78
  Spicy Vegetables with Rice, 69
  Spring Vegetable Paella, *68*, 69
  Squash-and-Lentil Risotto, 72
  Stuffed Cabbage, 62–63
  Stuffed Chiles with Walnut Sauce,
    84
  Swedish Summer Hash, 82, *83*
  Texas Red Beans and Rice, *59*, 61

Soups and Stews, 1–29
  Cabbage-Bean Soup with Rivels, 9
  Caribbean Stew with Pineapple
    Salsa, 22
  Curried Stew with Peanut Sauce,
    20–21
  Curried Yellow Split Pea Soup with
    Cilantro Cream, 18
  Easy Baked Stew, 19
  Garden Vegetable Stew, 23
  Gazpacho with Basil Crème Fraîche,
    16, *17*
  Lentil and Vegetable Stew, 19
  Lentil-Spinach Soup, 18
  Mediterranean Vegetable Soup, 14
  Pizza Soup, 4, *5*
  Roasted Vegetable Broth, 15
  Santa Fe Corn Chowder, 2
  Southern Lentils and Vegetables, 3, *6*
  Southwestern Black Bean Soup, 8
  Tortellini, Bean and Pesto Soup, *6*, 7
  Vegetable Broth, 14–15
  Vegetable Stew with Dill
    Dumplings, 21
  Wild Rice and Spinach au Gratin, 2
Southern Lentils and Vegetables, 3, *6*
Southern Peas and Greens, 34–35
Southwestern Black Bean Soup, 8
Southwestern Frittata, *92*, 93
Southwestern Wild Rice Salad, 112
Southwest Vegetable Stew with Corn
  Bread Topping, 36–37
Soybeans, 128
Spaghetti and Spicy Rice Balls, 81
Spiced Bulgur-and-Barley Balls, 78
Spicy Black Bean Stew, 20
Spicy Five-Pepper Spoon Bread, *56*, 57
Spicy Vegetables with Rice, 69
Spinach
  -Fennel Kugel, 52
  Frittata with Creole Sauce, 91
  Lasagne, Mushroom and, 51
  Pie, Phyllo and, 53
  Risotto Florentine, 76
  Soup, Lentil-, 18
Spring Vegetable Paella, *68*, 69
Squash-and-Lentil Risotto, 72
Stews. *See* Soups and Stews
Stir-fries
  Barley-Vegetable Sauté, 77
  Bean Cakes with Tomato Salsa,
    Sautéed, 70, *71*

Stir-fries (*continued*)
 Vegetable Sauté with Black Beans
  and Couscous, 63, *71*
Stuffed Cabbage, 62–63
Stuffed Chiles with Walnut Sauce, 84
Swedish Summer Hash, 82, *83*

T
Tabbouleh, Kasha, 109
Tabbouleh Casserole, 42
Texas Red Beans and Rice, *59*, 61
Tex-Mex Chile, 24
Tex-Mex Scrambled Eggs, 98
Textured Vegetable Protein, 128
Three-Bean Chile, 24
Three-Bean White Chile, 29
Three-Cheese Noodle Bake, 52
Time-Saving Tips, 94

Tomatillo Salsa, 29
Tomato Salsa, 70
Tortellini, Bean and Pesto Soup,
 6, 7
Tostadas, Mexican Pita, 127

V
Vegetable(s)
 Bake, Fall, 53
 Broth, 14–15
 Broth, Roasted, 15
 -Couscous Salad, 112
 Lentils and, Southern, 3, *6*
 Manicotti, 47
 Paella, Spring, *68*, 69
 Poached Eggs, *100*, 101
 Salad Sandwich, *116*, 117
 Sauté, Barley, 77

 Sauté with Black Beans and
  Couscous, 63, *71*
 Shepherd's Pie, 54
 Soup, Mediterranean, 14
 Stew, Lentils and, 19
 Stew with Dill Dumplings, 21
Vinaigrette Dressing, 113

W
Wheat Berry Salad, 113
Whole Wheat Fettucine with Spring
 Vegetables, 111, *113*
Wild Rice and Spinach au Gratin, 2
Winter Baked Pasta, *50*, 51
Winter Root Vegetable Casserole, 55

Z
Zucchini-Pinto Casserole, 35

Credits

GENERAL MILLS, INC.

Betty Crocker Food and Publications Center
   Director, Marcia Copeland
   Editor, Lori Fox
   Recipe Development, Hallie Harron, Julie Turnbull
   Food Stylists, Cindy Lund, Katie McElroy
Nutrition Department
   Nutritionist, Elyse A. Cohen, M.S., Nancy Holmes, R.D.
Photographic Services
   Photographer, Nanci Doonan Dixon